Praise for **The Empathy Dilemma**

"Maria Ross's *The Empathy Dilemma* is a refreshing and practical guide for leaders who want to make empathy more than just a buzzword. By focusing on self-awareness, self-care, clarity, decisiveness, and joy, Ross provides a holistic approach to empathetic leadership that is both inspiring and achievable."

DANIEL H. PINK, #1 *New York Times*–bestselling author of *Drive, When,* and *The Power of Regret*

"In *The Empathy Dilemma*, Maria Ross equips those of us managing workplace stress and burnout with the tools to develop an empathy practice that emphasizes much-needed self-care. Her Five Pillars of Effective Empathetic Leadership provide an invaluable framework for anyone wanting to cultivate a more empathetic and engaged culture without sacrificing high performance, clearly addressing the challenges of the post-COVID workplace."

TERRI GIVENS, professor at McGill University and author of *Radical Empathy*

"If you've made the mistake, like I have, of mixing up 'empathy' and 'being a pushover,' this book will save you. It will guide you on how to care and have boundaries, how to encourage and be a decisive leader."

MICHAEL BUNGAY STANIER, bestselling author of *The Coaching Habit*

"A vital, timely examination of modern workplace (dys)function, with real-world recipes for getting and keeping your team on track. Should be required reading for every manager."

JAY BAER, founder of Convince & Convert and author of *The Time to Win*

T0314418

"Empathy is a crucial skill for today's leaders. Command-and-control leadership is outdated, short-sighted, and unsustainable. Maria Ross smashes the perception that empathy and high performance cannot coexist. She shows you how to balance empathy and accountability to foster engaged, collaborative teams that deliver long-term results."

DORIE CLARK, *Wall Street Journal*-bestselling author of *The Long Game* and executive education faculty at Columbia Business School

"Packed with actionable insights and relatable stories, *The Empathy Dilemma* bridges the gap between leading with empathy and delivering results. Maria Ross busts common myths about empathy and offers a compelling road map for effective empathetic leadership that anyone can follow. This book is an essential guide for any leader who wants to build a thriving, connected, and high-performing organization in this new era of leadership."

RICH HUA, worldwide head of EPIC Leadership and founder of EQ@Amazon

"Leadership is finally waking up to our role as motivators and mentors. When our people thrive, so do our businesses. Our people come to work from different generations, ethnicities, and abilities. *The Empathy Dilemma* sets leaders up to successfully support all those needs and perspectives while delivering results—and without sacrificing their own mental health."

CHIP CONLEY, *New York Times*-bestselling author and founder of MEA, Modern Elder Academy

"Every leader should STOP and READ *The Empathy Dilemma*. It's the road map for how human-centered leadership should be done in today's fast-moving world."

RAMON RAY, publisher of ZoneofGenius.com

"Maria Ross gets us over the hurdle of inertia to a place of action. *The Empathy Dilemma* unpacks the barriers to empathy in the workplace and delivers a clear framework for how to move forward as leaders and as humans."

ROB VOLPE, Empathy Activist and author of
Tell Me More about That

"In *The Empathy Dilemma*, Maria Ross masterfully addresses the delicate balance leaders must strike between business needs and the well-being of their employees. Her personal journey, combined with extensive research and real-world examples, brings the Five Pillars of Effective Empathetic Leadership to life. A thought-provoking and insightful read for any leader looking to build a thriving, empathetic, and successful workplace culture."

DENISE BROUSSEAU, keynote speaker and
bestselling author of *Ready to Be a Thought Leader?*

"Maria Ross has laid out one of the great challenges of our times for leadership: how and when to use empathy without losing the plot. As much as we might want a purpose-led business with empathetic leadership, businesses that aren't profitable serve no purpose. As Ross explains, empathy is not about being weak and meek, or having always-on compassion. In *The Empathy Dilemma*, Ross nails it as she shows why and how leaders need to embrace empathy and ambition."

MINTER DIAL, award-winning author of
Heartificial Empathy and *You Lead*

"Empathy in business is needed more than ever in today's challenging world, and Maria Ross provides the necessary playbook that every leader must read."

SUSAN MCPHERSON, founder and CEO of McPherson Strategies
and author of *The Lost Art of Connecting*

"Leaders who believe that empathy sounds great in theory but won't make a dent for high-performance companies need to read *The Empathy Dilemma*. Likewise, ambitious employees who haven't integrated self-care practices—or joy!—into their professional lives have a lot to learn from Maria Ross. This book offers a road map for forward-thinking leaders who want to bring more humanity into the workplace."

ANITA NOWAK, author of *Purposeful Empathy* and on faculty with the McGill Executive Institute

"In *The Empathy Dilemma*, Maria Ross offers a compelling invitation and a clear road map to embrace empathy as a strength without sacrificing accountability. An essential book for today's leaders as they navigate the challenges of the twenty-first-century workplace."

MINETTE NORMAN, author of *The Boldly Inclusive Leader*

"In an age of 'quiet quitting,' empathy is more than a nice-to-have. Empathy expert Maria Ross shows us how to make our employees feel seen and valued as we build a joyful, successful culture."

MARTY NEUMEIER, cofounder of Level C and author of *The Brand Gap* and *Metaskills*

"The twenty-first century demands a new kind of leader. A leader focused on connection and collaboration, not command and control, in order to deliver exponential growth. *The Empathy Dilemma* is a must-read for those who falsely believe that leaders have to choose between people and performance. They absolutely do not. And Maria Ross shows you how it's possible."

ERICA DHAWAN, author of *Digital Body Language*

THE
EMPATHY
DILEMMA

How Successful Leaders Balance Performance, People, and Personal Boundaries

THE
EMPATHY
DILEMMA

MARIA ROSS

Cataloguing in publication information is available from Library and Archives Canada.
ISBN 978-1-77458-474-3 (paperback)
ISBN 978-1-77458-475-0 (ebook)

Page Two
pagetwo.com

Edited by Emily Schultz
Copyedited by Crissy Boylan
Proofread by Alison Strobel
Cover, interior design, and illustrations by Fiona Lee
Printed and bound in Canada by Friesens
Distributed in Canada by Raincoast Books
Distributed in the US and internationally by Macmillan

24 25 26 27 28   5 4 3 2 1

Red-Slice.com
TheEmpathyEdge.com

*For all the bold leaders embracing a more
human-centered approach AND performing
at the highest levels. Your choices impact
and influence your colleagues, families, and
communities. That's a win for us all.*

*And as ever, for Callum, my everyday empathy
practice partner. It's about the consistent attempt,
not perfection. As you grow up in this beautiful
yet often heartbreaking world, my work is
dedicated to helping you and so many others
understand how to embrace difference and find
connection. And how much richer your life will
be for it, my love.*

Also by Maria Ross

*The Empathy Edge: Harnessing the Value
of Compassion as an Engine for Success
(A Playbook for Brands, Leaders, and Teams)*

*Rebooting My Brain: How a
Freak Aneurysm Reframed My Life*

*Branding Basics for Small Business: How to
Create an Irresistible Brand on Any Budget*

The Juicy Guides for Entrepreneurs
(Ebook Series)

CONTENTS

INTRODUCTION

I T'S NOT just you. You are not imagining things.

It seems like everywhere we look in the world, from geo-political conflict down to workplace dynamics, people are having a hard time finding understanding and empathy. The headlines say it all:

Survey Shows Dramatic Drops in Empathy among Executives

Businessolver Study Reveals Decline in Workplace Empathy

The Empathy Gap between Workers and Companies Is Bigger Than Ever—but CEOs Just Don't Get It

Fewer Workers Say Their Employer Is Empathetic in 2022

Let's zoom into a real-world example, one I've seen far too often recently:

The vice-presidents and directors were exhausted.

Coaching a small departmental leadership group at a Fortune 500 financial services company, I could tell they were struggling. They had embraced people-centered leadership long before the pandemic. Their culture was known for being supportive and inclusive, and the company boasted many decades-long employees to prove how successful they had been.

But now, their empathetic leadership style was being met with resistance.

"Of course, we've bent over backwards and done so many things to help our teams through the pandemic," one of them told me. "But now that we need to ramp back into return-to-office for certain roles, we're being met with hostility and resistance. We've tried to sit down, listen to concerns, and explain the business reasons we need these particular roles back in the office and offered to find other ways to accommodate, but it doesn't seem to help. We're trying to be empathetic, but at some point, we must move the business forward."

As leaders, they were working more hours and spending more time than anticipated on these conversations. They felt overwhelmed and pushed beyond the breaking point, but they truly wanted to do right by their teams. They were burning themselves out trying to meet the demands of the business, while simultaneously trying to balance the needs of their people.

A lack of empathy did not seem to be the issue. To me, it seemed they had been conflating empathy with a need for more trust (so workers knew managers had their best interests at heart as they made these difficult decisions) and better role fit (did the company still align with the values and needs of these workers?).

Work had changed. People's lives had changed. And perhaps the company's goals and what these workers needed from their jobs no longer matched up. More importantly, perhaps these leaders were sacrificing their own well-being and boundaries in the name of empathy. Maybe they were not really practicing effective empathy, but something else entirely.

After hearing this weary tale from so many well-intentioned leaders squeezed from both ends, I knew I had to write this book. For them. Maybe for you too.

All across the globe, organizations are becoming more human-centric. They've jettisoned old paradigms of success that center on endless overtime and constant employee sacrifice. They've tied success to purpose and workforce morale, and they've helped people balance personal and professional needs as their priorities change. They've made shifts that are both necessary and positive.

With those shifts have come changes in workplace culture, benefits offerings, even job duties. And when those social shifts collide with accelerants like the COVID-19 pandemic, employee expectations begin to morph. Compassionate policies that were once actively appreciated become taken for granted. Leniency is expected instead of requested. Workers come to believe that they inherently deserve perks, flexibility, and treatment that was once reserved for emergencies or rewards. Workers feel entitled to special treatment at all times and under all circumstances.

And because of this, business leaders are starting to see the dark side of empathy.

In some cases, people-focused work policies have skewed employee expectations. Workers across industries now resist workplace citizenship behaviors: they refuse to stay late, show up early, or attend non-mandatory meetings. "That's not my job" has become the new office-wide mantra. In response, leaders and fully engaged workers must do more, work more, and facilitate more just to keep their companies moving forward. And if they press their disengaged team members to perform during crunch times, market downturns, or client emergencies, they face blowback.

Empathy has been weaponized. Employers who commit to building compassionate workplaces feel like they must say yes to every employee request or risk watching helplessly as more people embrace "quiet quitting." Asking for out-of-scope project support, even on an emergency basis, seems to be completely off the table.

How can leaders hold people accountable and set high expectations without being treated like villains? Is the answer to turn back the clock and reinstate iron-fist bossism, à la Elon Musk at Tesla and X (formerly Twitter)?

In a word: *no*.

I wrote this book to prevent this bad situation from getting worse. And I wrote this book to support leaders who want to be more human but are also struggling to get work done.

What We Risk

So why are leaders who believe in empathy struggling or even beginning to flip-flop? When people are scared or unsure, they run back to what they know. That's what some leaders are doing in today's post-pandemic workplace.

And it's pissing me off.

Today, as the pandemic fades and a recession looms, many employers are back to their old ways—reacting to market conditions, sometimes haphazardly and sometimes without much compassion. Being an empathetic leader does not mean you have to be "the cool parent," lower your standards, or fix everything for everyone. As journalist Rebecca Knight wrote for *Business Insider*, "Managers need to be empathetic... but they must also provide workers with guidance and direction and not shield them from economic realities."

First, it's bang-on that the pandemic forced leaders and companies to find humanity. We were in a global crisis then, and in many ways we still are now. All we have is our humanity. People's lives were turned upside down. Of course we turned to compassionate leadership. To empathy. We *had* to.

But this was not a new trend that just popped up. The signs all pointed to a new model of leadership before anyone had ever uttered the phrase *herd immunity*. Study after study showed that the industrial revolution models of leadership were having less of an effect. That worker desires, combined with technology and transparency, demanded a new leadership model: one based on collaboration and connection. A more human workplace. And the rewards? *Huge*. Increased productivity, engagement, retention, top talent attraction, morale, innovation, performance, customer satisfaction. The data existed way before COVID began.

The pandemic just accelerated the need to adopt these new models. There was no other way forward but to adapt.

Now that we are coming out of the pandemic, though, there's backlash. Back to bossism. Command and control. As if the thinking is "They had their fun being treated like human beings, but now it's back to work."

It's maddening.

Second, only leaders who don't understand what is truly meant by empathy hold this position. Empathy is not about caving in to unrealistic demands, letting workers do whatever they want to do, or accepting slipping performance. It's about listening, getting curious, sitting with someone's struggle or perspective, and finding a way forward.

Even at companies that pay lip service to compassionate culture, I've found far too many people believe that empathetic leadership is an either/or proposition when it's really both/and. We can embrace empathy *and* ambition, compassion *and* competition, kindness *and* high performance. I sign off every episode of my podcast, *The Empathy Edge*, with the mantra "Cash flow, creativity, and compassion are not mutually exclusive" because it is possible. So I've dedicated myself to sharing, teaching, and inspiring the both/and philosophy. Proving that leaders who adopt *healthy* empathetic habits with their teams can still expect high performance, set boundaries, and avoid burnout. They can do so *if* they have the right foundation to embrace empathy in a healthy way.

And so can you. This book will give you that foundation.

How This Book Works

I present empathy keynotes and workshops all over the world for organizations big and small, so I have my finger on the pulse of the emerging empathy crisis. As I mentioned earlier, I'm seeing business leaders so panicked by shifting workplace dynamics that they're reverting to harsher and less people-centric tactics simply to get their numbers back in the black. They believe that abandoning workplace empathy is the only way to boost productivity and efficiency.

And major news outlets aren't doing anything to help alleviate that fear. Case in point: a 2023 *Fortune* cover story that reads "Efficiency Is In. Is Empathy Out?"

On the flip side, leaders are striving to keep empathy alive, but the effort is causing them to burn out on a personal level. They're absorbing extra work, struggling to meet an array of new employee demands, facing weaponized empathy, and feeling forced to lower their performance standards. Dedicated managers and executives everywhere are determined to maintain compassionate work environments, but they're increasingly unsure how to do so while remaining sane and stable themselves.

We don't have to go back. We can go forward in a way that helps leaders take care of themselves and still leads to phenomenal success. We don't have to burn out. We can create balance between empathy and healthy boundaries, so everyone thrives. I want to help both leaders and employees understand how empathy works, how it can benefit them, and how to ensure it remains an equitable, two-way street.

Empathy is more about mutual understanding and support than it is about acquiescence.

So how should empathy work at work? It's sometimes a delicate question. In the chapters that follow, I offer guidance on the healthy and productive ways leaders can deal with the unique challenges they're facing in trying to balance empathy and performance.

Most of that guidance is grounded in the **Five Pillars of Effective Empathetic Leadership.** These are traits and behaviors that I've seen modeled by many empathetically healthy business leaders. Common threads I see over and over again in the successful empathetic leaders I interview and advise. I'm introducing you to them here for the first time but will dive deeper into their details throughout the chapters to come.

1 **Self-awareness:** Understanding your own strengths, blind spots, emotions, leadership style, and triggers. And helping your team members understand theirs.

2 **Self-care:** Enforcing strong boundaries, taking time to recharge, delegating, resting, and stewarding one's own mental health as a leader.

3 **Clarity:** Ensuring everyone is on the exact same page through clear communication, expectations, feedback, and understanding of job roles, all of which roll up to an actionable mission statement and meaningful company values.

4 **Decisiveness:** Taking thoughtful but swift action that doesn't leave people hanging, addressing issues before they fester, quickly synthesizing input and perspectives to make wise choices, and practicing radical and kind honesty.

5 **Joy:** Ensuring people enjoy their work, encouraging work friendships, and creating a thriving culture even when the work itself is challenging.

See how none of these pillars includes "Being a total pushover" or "Never asking for overtime"? Empathy is more about mutual understanding and support than it is about acquiescence. In a work setting, it means getting to know each other on a personal level, as human beings, to build trust and mutual respect. It means ensuring everyone understands each other, their roles and goals, and the fundamental reasons they're being asked to perform specific tasks. All in an effort not to people-please but to help teams thrive and do their best work. Without that understanding, it's easy to conflate compassion with pliability.

In the pages that follow, we'll explore where we go wrong in our empathetic efforts and complicating factors like generational mindsets, philosophical differences, and diverse life experiences. There are a lot of myths about the very idea of empathy, and I'll unpack those, as well as share insights from some of the most successful leaders using and studying empathy today. And we'll talk about how to be empathetic while setting boundaries, expecting excellence, and avoiding burnout, all through the lens of these Five Pillars.

I still believe we can leverage empathy to achieve radical success, but we have to be smart about it. We must take care of ourselves as leaders so we can continue making the transformation that's already in process. And we can strike that vital balance between empathy and accountability.

So let's dig in and find out how you can continue to be compassionate without sacrificing productivity, profit, or purpose.

PART I

WHY WORKPLACE EMPATHY FEELS HARD

WHAT IS EMPATHY IN A WORK CONTEXT?

No, You Won't Have to Cry on
the Floor with Your Team.
Yes, You Will Get Work Done.

---

*"True power does not amass through
the pain and suffering of others."*
JOY HARJO, former U.S. poet laureate,
A Map to the Next World

E MPATHY IS a critically important concept in modern life, but it's also a nuanced and complex one. And one that, unfortunately, many leaders get wrong, as these anonymized quotes from some of my past workshop attendees illustrate.

"If I'm empathetic at work, my team will walk all over me."
Vice-president

"Empathy will just make everything take longer. Too much coddling, sorting out personal preferences and issues."
Senior director

"If I'm too empathetic, I may lose control and the work will suffer."
Group manager

Between 2016 and 2019 when I was researching my previous book, *The Empathy Edge*, every single expert I interviewed had a slightly different definition of empathy. So did all the experts and pundits I quoted. Former U.S. president Barack Obama offered a great definition of empathy in a college commencement speech he gave several years ago. He described it as "seeing the world through the eyes of those who are different from us." And Simon Sinek, leadership expert and author of *Start with Why*, insists that empathy is the number one tool in a leader's toolbox. He says it's the ability to recognize and share other people's feelings.

And even if you look at the definition of empathy over time, it has changed dramatically from the 1700s to today. I believe the wide variety of conflicting and convoluted ideas about the concept are contributing to the escalating tensions I've seen between leaders and their teams.

So before we start exploring how empathy functions at work and how to sustain it without becoming a doormat, let's talk about what empathy really *means*.

After hundreds of interviews, talks, and hours of research, the definition I want to propose to you and invite you to embrace in an organizational context is this: empathy is being willing and able to see, understand, and (where appropriate) feel another person's perspective and to use that information to act compassionately.

This definition encompasses a few related concepts that can be especially useful to leaders. First, you don't have to feel exactly what another person is feeling to infuse empathy into your interactions, which is incredibly helpful in making empathy feel more possible and easier to access.

Second, while empathy is a great place to start, it's just a start. If you don't take action on it, it can seem like a wasted mindset. Moving from empathy (imagining, feeling) to compassion (action) is especially important in business settings. That action can take the form of many things: how you communicate, what questions you should be prepared to answer, how to support someone through a difficult conversation, and when you need to offer space and actively listen. Your action *definitely* does not have to take the form of "doing exactly what the other person wants."

And third, empathy can be viewed as a method of information gathering, a way to understand where the other person is coming from so you can respond accordingly. It's like a nonjudgmental and caring form of research about the context and ideas of the people around you.

The empathy definition I've refined also reflects the two types of empathy that people commonly experience.

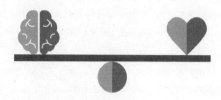

- **Cognitive empathy:** This is the empathy that uses your brain first, before your heart gets involved. You might be imagining what something might be like for someone else, even if you've never experienced it yourself. You're asking yourself, "What would it be like for me if I were in their position?" That's a cognitive exercise and can often, but not always, lead to...

- **Emotional empathy:** This is feeling, echoing, or mirroring the emotions that someone else is feeling. It's empathy using your heart. When someone cries and you start to tear up yourself, that's the brain's good old mirror neurons in full effect. A husband feels his own version of labor pains when his wife is in labor. Someone feels anxious and stressed, and your blood pressure starts to rise just listening to them explain why. It might occur because one person has experienced the exact same thing as another, or because they've experienced something similar and can easily recall the associated feelings.

Rob Volpe, Empathy Activist, author of the award-winning book *Tell Me More about That: Solving the Empathy Crisis One Conversation at a Time*, and founder of consumer insights research firm Ignite 360, said, "People often go straight to the 'feeling' side of empathy, at the expense of the cognitive, perspective-taking side. It's cognitive empathy that is used in most of our interactions with people other than those we are closest to—the clerk at the store, the colleague in the office, the client on the phone, the stranger on the street."

Volpe believes that our fundamental misunderstanding of empathy is a product of decades of societal programming about how people are expected to show up in the workplace. All the way back to Dickens's character of Ebenezer Scrooge, our culture has characterized business leaders and bosses as detached, relentless, and laser-focused on profits.

"We have taught people that CEOs are supposed to be cold and decisive, that there's no room for empathetic leaders," Volpe explained. "Men especially are supposed to show up in the workplace as hard decision-makers. Look at the business leaders that we've put up on a pedestal: they're the cutthroat titans of industry. And they're the ones who are informing our ideas about what the workplace is supposed to look like, and how leaders function in the workplace."

This can change, of course. These paradigms are not laws of physics. We humans created these models, which means we can shift them.

And shifting them can be as simple as learning what empathy truly means and putting it into action. Both cognitive and emotional empathy can lead to compassion, and as I mentioned above, compassion is empathy in action; it's being moved to act based on the information you're getting cognitively and emotionally. Just knowing that can inform our words and choices as leaders and guide us toward fostering truly empathetic work cultures.

Now that we've got a sense of what empathy is, let's talk about what it *isn't*.

Examining Empathy Myths

My work consulting with and speaking to clients has taught me that it's equally important to understand what empathy is *not*. There are quite a few empathy myths that need busting, and I do my best to ensure they're smashed to smithereens.

Empathy Myth 1: Empathy Means "Being Nice"

Not so! There are lots of nice people in our workplaces. That doesn't mean they see things from our point of view or connect with us emotionally. It might just mean they bake delicious cookies and bring them to work. Creating an empathetic culture means more than just hiring a bunch of really nice people.

Empathy Myth 2: Empathy Means Caving In to Any and All Demands

Thankfully, no. Caving in to unreasonable demands is often the opposite of empathy. I get lots of sighs of relief from seasoned executives when I say this because—especially when it comes to intergenerational conflict—so many leaders assume acquiescence *is* empathy. We need to remember that you can see someone's point of view and understand their context and *still* make a tough business decision that might negatively affect them, like a layoff or reorg.

Empathy Myth 3: Empathy Runs in a Single Direction from Leaders to Workers

Are leaders the only ones who need to learn and express empathy for their staff? Absolutely not. It's a two-way street, and all parties should bear that in mind. Consider mid-level managers who are being squeezed from both sides, balancing the business needs from on high with the individual needs of their team members. If they experience empathy from their

Empathy is being willing and able to see, understand, and (where appropriate) feel another person's perspective and to use that information to act compassionately.

bosses but not from their direct reports, they may end up feeling demonized and isolated. Strengthening empathy is everyone's job, and it must be modeled and supported.

Empathy Myth 4: Empathy Means Agreement

Especially in work situations, this isn't always the case. You can have empathy for someone and also have a productive dialogue about the points on which you disagree. And do so without trying to persuade them to your point of view.

If you don't believe me about this fourth myth, I'd urge you to look into the work of Edwin Rutsch. He is the founding director of The Center for Building a Culture of Empathy and is now the founding director of The Empathy Center in Santa Barbara, California. He and a team of partners conduct training with people from all over the world on a facilitation technique called empathy circles. Rutsch believes that the empathy circle (based on mutual active listening) is the foundational practice of the empathy movement, just as meditation is the foundational practice of the compassion movement.

While this technique can be applied to any discussion or topic where there are multiple points of view, he has facilitated empathy circles at divisive political rallies over the last few years and gotten people from opposite ends of the political spectrum to engage in civil, respectful discussion with each other. Many participants walk away with an understanding of their shared humanity, even if they haven't moved an inch on their political views. Rutsch's work proves that the goal of empathy is connection, not necessarily conversion.

If, in the past, you've conflated empathy with niceness, caving, or agreement, don't beat yourself up. People across industries and at all levels are doing the same thing every day, which is one reason empathetic leaders are struggling.

An executive I interviewed while doing research for this book shared a story with me that perfectly illustrates the risks of assuming that empathy means giving in to any and all demands.

Let's meet Janet (not her real name), a senior director at a large technology company. Empathetic by nature, Janet supported her team throughout the pandemic, ensuring they had what they needed to not just be successful but also take care of themselves. A newer person on her team showed signs of struggling early on. Janet went out of her way to give extra training and guidance to this team member, and her other employees also offered their expertise and support. But this new person, whom we'll call Alex, continually did her work incorrectly. And extremely slowly.

Alex had been open about her struggles with mental health, so Janet understood completely when she requested time off under the Family and Medical Leave Act (FMLA). But when Alex returned, she told Janet, "I'm not doing well with your management style." Janet tried to make some accommodations, but shortly after that confrontation Alex began avoiding her. On days the two of them were scheduled to meet, Alex would excuse herself from the meeting early, not show up at all, or call in sick for the whole day.

"There were accommodations that were requested along the way, and I always said yes," Janet told me. "Things like taking an extra hour break during the day. I always tried to say, 'Do what you need to do, but we still do need to get the work done.' The problem was that the work was not getting done."

Alex continually failed to deliver and always found a way to blame someone or something else other than herself. She framed her own missed deadlines and mistakes as *things that happened to her* instead of things she could influence. Alex's avoidance of her meetings with Janet made it impossible for Janet to discern the true cause of this underperformance so she could offer the right support. If the two of them could have talked, they might have found ways for Alex to refocus her efforts, get the support she needed, or even switch positions within the company so she could do work that suited her better. But Alex's refusal to speak with her boss meant Janet couldn't help her succeed.

It also made Janet feel like a failure.

"It was a tough battle," she said. "And it made me feel like I was not being a good manager, even though I was doing what I was supposed to do. I'm such a people person, and I wanted to make her feel supported. I kept second-guessing myself. I thought, 'What else should I be doing? What else could I say? How do I turn this around?'"

Even to an objective observer, this tricky situation was certainly not Janet's fault; Alex put up multiple barriers to the two of them reaching a mutually beneficial arrangement. Alex also made it nearly impossible for Janet to practice our definition of empathy. Without two-way communication, Janet couldn't see, understand, or feel Alex's perspective and use that information to act compassionately. But if Janet had been able to set stronger boundaries with Alex, offer corrective action earlier, or open a discussion on moving Alex to a different role, this drawn-out conflict could have been curtailed. (All examples of the Clarity Pillar, which I'll discuss in Chapter 6.) Instead, Janet suffered, Alex suffered, and in the end Alex quit. Janet's efforts to train, support, and accommodate her were wasted. Not to mention the toll this took on the entire team.

See how this type of behavior is woefully counterproductive? Misunderstanding empathy in a work context isn't just an issue of semantics. When business leaders believe they must be universally agreeable, it impacts their efficacy and well-being.

Even with a solid definition in place, it can be hard to envision modeling empathetic leadership when you're operating in a high-pressure workplace on a daily basis. What does seeing, understanding, and feeling another person's perspective look like in a performance review? A board meeting? A difficult discussion about a missed deadline? Or if you're worried that your current leadership style is drifting away from empathy, how can you get yourself back on track?

Taking things on a case-by-case basis works under many circumstances, but in this situation it's a recipe for burnout. It means constantly improvising and hoping you don't inadvertently establish a harmful or counterproductive precedent. Instead, I believe modern leaders need high-level, broadly applicable guidelines to help them shape their policies and guide their choices. And I have a few to suggest.

Through years of study and hundreds of interviews, I've determined that empathetically healthy business leaders share five key behaviors and mindsets. I call them the Five Pillars of Effective Empathetic Leadership, and you first saw them in the introduction to this book. Let's revisit them again now, and dive into their specific relevance.

Pillar 1: Self-Awareness

What Is Self-Awareness?

Understanding your own emotions, leadership style, and triggers. And helping your team members understand theirs.

Why Is Self-Awareness Important?

No one leads in a vacuum. Your style, preferences, pet peeves, needs, and strengths as a leader will influence every single interaction you have at work. And yet many leaders don't take the time to understand themselves fully and completely.

Self-awareness helps you to understand complaints and constructive feedback, know when you might need help navigating a situation, and take accountability for your actions.

What Does Self-Awareness Look Like in Practice?

Emotional intelligence expert Daniel Goleman has said, "If your emotional abilities aren't in hand, if you don't have self-awareness, if you are not able to manage your distressing emotions, if you can't have empathy and have effective relationships, then no matter how smart you are, you are not going to get very far."

And when I interviewed Rhonda George-Denniston, chief learning and development officer, TBWA\Worldwide, for my podcast, *The Empathy Edge*, she supported this, saying:

> Self-awareness is one of the most important traits to becoming an effective leader today. Before you can lead others, you need deep awareness of your own values. You really have to know how you're showing up for others so you can either dial it up or dial it back. You have to know how you're received and perceived by others.
>
> At my company, we work with world-class coaches to help our people develop their leadership skills and identify whether or not they're sucking the air out of the room. We also encourage them to seek feedback from others as part of their growth strategy and then take action on the input they receive. And we offer various diagnostic and psychometric tools, so our leaders get insights into and data about who they are and their personal strengths. That definitely helps them to create a map for who they want to become at any level. Even the most experienced leaders can benefit from understanding a little bit more about themselves, getting a little bit more insight into their leadership styles. And that includes both strengths and blind spots.

Pillar 2: Self-Care

What Is Self-Care?

Enforcing strong boundaries, taking time to recharge, delegating, resting, and stewarding one's own mental health as a leader.

Why Is Self-Care Important?

Depleted leaders are ineffective leaders. It can be tempting to shoulder additional burdens in the name of empathy, but in the end, you are doing yourself a disservice. True empathy means not simply treating others as we would like to be treated (normally cited as the Golden Rule) but, as discussed in my previous book, *The Empathy Edge*, empathy requires the Platinum Rule: Do unto others as *they* would have done unto them. And we can't even see what that is for someone else if we're too focused on self-preservation. It means getting your own house in order so you can meet other perspectives with curiosity rather than defensiveness or fear. Self-care helps you avoid burnout as a leader, balance everyone's workloads and time with your own, and model healthy behaviors.

What Does Self-Care Look Like in Practice?

When I chatted with women's leadership coach Jamie Greenwood, she pointed out that self-care is often frowned upon in business settings:

> It's deeply culturally uncomfortable to be kind to ourselves. We wrap it up in our productivity, saying, "This is going to slow me down; this is going to make me a weaker leader." So to make space for it in your own life, you have to be a bit of a rebel.
>
> I know that anytime I try to be empathetic toward someone else while I'm feeling constricted, my empathy toward them is nowhere near what it needs to be. When we

can first start with ourselves, that impacts how we are with others. We need to be able to say, "This is a moment of suffering; this is hard. I'd like to be kind and tender to myself at this moment." When we can feel and access tenderness within ourselves, we can then offer that to someone else much more easily. Especially people who struggle with empathy—who want it in their lives but don't quite know how to weave it in—I recommend being kind to yourself. After that, it's a natural outflow to other people.

Pillar 3: Clarity

What Is Clarity?
Ensuring everyone is on the exact same page through clear communication, expectations, feedback, and understanding of job roles, all of which roll up to an actionable mission statement and meaningful company values.

Why Is Clarity Important?
Resentments build where misunderstandings thrive. One of the biggest reasons leaders and workers butt heads is lack of communication on mission, roles, and responsibilities. When people know what's expected of them—including in emergencies and on an as-needed basis—they are less likely to become disgruntled. Clarity helps people feel seen, heard, and valued; reduces the likelihood of conflict; and enables everyone to work together more effectively.

What Does Clarity Look Like in Practice?
Business builder and C-suite technology executive Dave Zinman knows from experience that empathy and clarity go hand in hand. He told me how thoughtful and thorough communication can completely transform the dynamics between leaders and workers.

"People need a very clear understanding of their roles, what is required of those roles, and what is expected of them," he told me in an interview.

Everyone needs clarity on what the leader has promised and committed to. I have this vision that all leaders would start creating something that goes beyond a job description: a "rules of engagement" declaration that people talk through when they begin a job or start a new role. It wouldn't just say, "Here are all the tasks I need you to do." It would include things like, "We will do our best to ensure that nobody works on weekends; however, we expect your support if there's a crisis." Clarity like this could eliminate arguments like, "You're not respecting my boundaries because you told me I'd never work on a weekend." The rules of engagement would create much-needed clarity by digging deeper into how work gets done, how we treat each other, how and when you can advance in the organization, and what might be required of you on occasion. You'll see some examples of this in Chapter 6.

Pillar 4: Decisiveness

What Is Decisiveness?
Taking thoughtful but swift action that doesn't leave people hanging, addressing issues before they fester, quickly synthesizing input and perspectives to make wise choices, and practicing radical and kind honesty.

Why Is Decisiveness Important?
Keeping people in limbo is one of the least empathetic things a leader can do! It can feel risky to commit to decisions quickly, but dragging your feet will only erode trust. This doesn't, however, mean you just make decisions alone, like a dictator. Soliciting input and addressing choices, action plans, and pending questions as soon as possible is the most

The goal
of empathy is
connection,
not necessarily
conversion.

compassionate way to operate. Doing this shows your team members that you respect their input and that you want them to know how to best move forward. It helps them fully understand what's happening around them. Decisiveness helps leaders maintain momentum, cultivate trust among teams, and build a culture of open and consistent honesty.

What Does Decisiveness Look Like in Practice?

Rich Hua, worldwide head of EPIC Leadership and founder of EQ@Amazon, has created employee emotional intelligence initiatives at Oracle and Amazon. In a video interview, he highlighted some of the empathetic leadership practices at his client companies.

"The interesting thing about [Amazon's internal] leadership principles is that they have emotional intelligence implicit in them. For example, one of them is 'Earned trust,' and it says, 'Leaders listen attentively, speak candidly, and treat others respectfully. They are vocally self-critical even when doing so is awkward or embarrassing.' There's another one that says, 'Have backbone. Disagree and commit.' And that says that you respectfully challenge decisions when you disagree, even when doing so is uncomfortable or exhausting."

"Disagree and commit" is a policy that has gained traction beyond Amazon to keep companies moving forward even when opinions clash. It is both a fantastic example of decisiveness in practice and a great reminder that committing to a path doesn't require full consensus. Sometimes, it falls to a business leader to make a tough call and plow ahead despite naysayers. They can and should do so *as long as* they first encourage people to share ideas and bring up good points to factor in to the decisions and then clearly explain why and how the decision was made.

Pillar 5: Joy

What Is Joy?

Ensuring people enjoy their work, encouraging work friendships, and creating a thriving culture even when the work itself is challenging.

Why Is Joy Important?

Multiple studies have shown that when people enjoy their work, it leads to lower rates of turnover, higher productivity, increased company profits, and more loyalty to the employer. But beyond these pragmatic reasons, empathetic business leaders generally want their teams to be happy, successful, and fulfilled to buoy the overall culture. A joyful work culture breeds trust to collaborate better, innovate, and take risks. It empowers people to have each other's backs. And as the late Herb Kelleher, cofounder and former CEO of Southwest Airlines, famously said, happy employees mean happy customers.

What Does Joy Look Like in Practice?

Gallup research has repeatedly shown that work friendships are linked to higher employee engagement and job success. Recently, the company published an article urging businesses to build cultures that foster work friendships and offered tips for leaders. According to Gallup,

> Leaders are facing significant challenges supporting connections and friendships among a physically distant workforce... managers are responsible for promoting a local team atmosphere that encourages trust and collaboration. Wherever possible, managers should remove constraints to socialization and create an atmosphere where employees feel free and encouraged to connect and show support... Managers and leaders can also support connections by making time to talk to employees themselves. For instance, a 15-minute

manager-employee conversation might highlight ways to pair team members on new tasks to promote friendships. Frequent conversations can also reveal barriers that preclude friendships at work.

You're going to see the Five Pillars frequently as you make your way through this book. In the chapters to come, we'll discuss ways that you can incorporate these mindsets into your leadership practice while still setting healthy boundaries, expecting excellence, and avoiding burnout. I'll give you lots of examples and tactics so you can determine how best to fortify the Five Pillars of Effective Empathetic Leadership in your own life.

I truly believe that you'll need them. Especially since the work landscape has been shifting for some time and is likely to continue shifting in the future.

The New Era of Work

On that note, however, I want to be clear: the future of work is already here. It's not some far-off horizon that we're drifting toward; it's the reality of the present. We are living right now in the new era of work, and leaders are feeling the shift in some challenging ways.

Managers and leaders are being squeezed. They are being asked to become everything to everyone all at once: high performers, implementers, "therapists," diversity champions, mentors, motivators, and drivers of peerless results.

None of this in and of itself is bad ... but it's a lot to take on. These leaders are being asked to do all of their own work *and* spend time caring about the mental well-being and career development of their employees. Their team members are plying them with questions, accommodation requests, and concerns. Their bosses are pressuring them to meet business goals and drive market performance. It's a high-pressure juggling act that many find difficult to master.

Remote work and hybrid environments add an extra layer of complexity. How do managers and leaders oversee workflow? How do they keep team collaboration alive? How do they accommodate different needs and experiences to create an inclusive environment that may not please everyone? Business leaders like you are working to connect, engage, and have difficult conversations, while supporting leadership decisions from above and adapting to organizational shifts. This leaves little room for building a life outside work and little energy for family, friends, and rejuvenating activities.

Many leaders are choosing one of two paths. Some are pleasing everyone on their team so they don't lose good talent but then working extra hours themselves, delivering less than stellar quality work, and steadily burning themselves out. Others are falling back on old, rigid leadership paradigms to survive. They're reverting to "command and control" in an attempt to forestall their own nervous breakdowns. I know this behavior well. It's what I fall back on with my young son when he's dawdled so long getting ready that we are running late. Once I feel like I've tried every technique in the book, I resort to commands and threats so we can just get out of the damn house!

Neither path is ideal, but the second one has led to some truly disastrous outcomes in workplaces. Here's one directly from the headlines.

In September 2020, Coinbase CEO Brian Armstrong chose the "command and control" path when he banned discussion of politics at his company, offering severance packages to employees unable or unwilling to abide by the new rules. Five percent of the company's staff—a total of sixty people—quit within two weeks of the announcement.

Coinbase is an exchange for buying and selling cryptocurrency, and Armstrong maintained that the financial services company needed to refocus on its mission. In his blog post announcing the new "apolitical" culture, he wrote, "Coinbase's mission is to create an open financial system for the world. This means we want to use cryptocurrency to bring economic freedom to people all over the world."

Alternative financial systems are, by their very nature, political. Using crypto to create global economic freedom is an *extremely* political goal.

So what did these new restrictions actually mean? In theory, everyone from leaders to employees would be subject to the same "apolitical" rules. In practice, however, Coinbase employees saw:

- Elimination of the popular all-hands format in which staff could openly question executives.

- Armstrong retweeting an article from Soylent founder Rob Rhinehart titled "Why I Am Voting for Kanye West" and posting a photo of himself with then speaker of the house Nancy Pelosi.

- Their company go public as a direct listing, instead of the traditional IPO path, ensuring mostly high-net-worth investors could participate.

- Requests for employees to delete posts questioning the "apolitical" policy from the all-company Slack channel.

Clearly, Armstrong and other leaders were perfectly happy to bend the rules for their own needs, while enforcing them strictly among the rest of the workforce.

Even before the September 2020 announcement and its fallout, Coinbase struggled to show consistent empathy for its workforce. A total of fifteen Black employees resigned due to racist or discriminatory treatment between 2018 and 2019. Leaders removed office signs that invited people to use any bathroom where they felt comfortable. At an all-hands meeting in 2020 after George Floyd was killed by Minneapolis police, some Black employees talked about their experiences at Coinbase. *Wired*'s Gregory Barber wrote, "Black employees described feeling invisible at a company that had not publicly acknowledged their pain, and like 'a clown' for trying to defend Coinbase's inaction to outsiders." Armstrong's response to his employees' openness was a belated Twitter thread, followed by total retreat from the charged discussion. Just a few months later came the blog post introducing Coinbase's official "apolitical" policy and then the offer of buyouts.

As you might expect, some of Armstrong's peers were outraged. For example, Laszlo Bock, CEO and cofounder of Humu, wrote, "By mandating that employees keep politics, activism, and their personal beliefs completely out of the workplace, leaders ensure that many people, particularly members of historically underrepresented groups, silently bear a tremendous emotional weight."

But plenty of others applauded Armstrong's vision. A few even followed in his footsteps. And as time flies by us, I expect many more companies to turn back the clock and reinstate iron-fist bossism. (Looking at you, Jamie Dimon.)

But there is a third path! You can embrace empathy as your core value while simultaneously establishing clear cultural norms and guideposts that protect leaders and team members alike. The third path—the one we'll follow in this book—enables business leaders to tap into the best of empathy without shouldering the risks.

This path sounds simple enough, right? And yet we are still struggling.

In the next chapter, we'll examine the motivations and behaviors that lead us astray even when we do our best to leverage empathy mindfully and strategically.

Chapter Highlights

- Our working definition of empathy: empathy is being willing and able to see, understand, and (where appropriate) feel another person's perspective and to use that information to act compassionately.

- Cognitive and emotional empathy are different, but both are equally important and can lead to compassionate action.

- Common misconceptions about empathy, such as it being solely about being nice or always agreeing with others, can prevent leaders from leveraging it effectively.

- Recognizing that empathy is a reciprocal process that should be practiced by both leaders and employees helps create a harmonious work environment.

- The five foundational pillars that underpin effective empathy in leadership are self-awareness, self-care, clarity, decisiveness, and joy.

WHERE WE GO WRONG WITH WORKPLACE EMPATHY

Empathy Doesn't Always Mean What You Think It Means

"*It's an unbelievable responsibility to influence decisions, shareholder value, and, most important to me, people's careers and livelihoods.*"
ANDREA JUNG, president and CEO of Grameen America and former chairwoman and CEO of Avon Products

D URING THE 2000s' Silicon Valley tech bust and its many dotcom failures, mergers, and acquisitions, I was laid off. More than once during that roller coaster of a market. If you've ever been laid off yourself, you know that the process is always a painful one. Even companies with seasoned, savvy leaders often struggle to let people go with grace and compassion. Knowing that layoff notifications are emotionally loaded when they're made and endlessly scrutinized after the fact makes these announcements even harder for C-suite members to compose with confidence, much less empathy.

Which can lead to disaster.

In January 2023, cloud computing company PagerDuty found itself embroiled in one such disaster. CEO Jennifer Tejada chose to announce that the company was cutting 7 percent of its staff via a lengthy 1,671-word email. The email was written in a decidedly upbeat tone and buried the layoff announcement about halfway through, instead of leading with it.

Notifying people of layoffs in writing is a decision that some might say lacks an empathetic touch to begin with... but wait, there's more.

In an attempt to underline her belief that PagerDuty was a leader in building an equitable world, Tejada included a quote from Dr. Martin Luther King Jr. in this particular email.

"I am reminded in moments like this, of something Martin Luther King said, that 'the ultimate measure of a [leader] is not where [they] stand in the moments of comfort and convenience, but where [they] stand in times of challenge and controversy,'" she wrote on January 24, 2023. She also added that she was excited to appoint a new executive and reorganize her customer-success team.

The announcement was met with criticism both inside and outside of PagerDuty. People were rankled by the tone, the failure to share layoff information at the very beginning, and the inappropriateness of invoking Dr. King's work in the context of a corporate mass firing. I'd add that Tejada's note to her staff centered the narrative on her as a leader and not on the people who would be most acutely affected by this business decision. In all likelihood she was *trying to be empathetic* when she wrote to her workforce: to bolster optimism as a counterbalance to the bad news, to praise the company overall for its equitable policies so her people knew she was proud of them. But her efforts came off as clumsy and misguided.

Tejada later apologized for her misstep, as she should have. But she also deserves our empathy. She was hardly the first leader to attempt empathy and fall short, and she certainly won't be the last.

To help you avoid joining these ranks, let's dive into the common ways that business leaders try and fail to act with empathy.

Empathy Hijacking

Power hierarchies are inherent to corporate culture, but many leaders have become increasingly uncomfortable with them. They know that team members may resent or disdain these rankings of influence, so leaders attempt to downplay their standing. This often manifests as attempts at camaraderie; leaders try to show that they "get it" and understand their direct reports' pain points because they've had the very same experiences themselves.

This can be dangerous territory and often leads to what I've termed "empathy hijacking."

We've all done it at some point. In a well-intentioned effort to connect, we listen to someone else's plight and then share our own related story. We're trying to illustrate how deeply and personally we understand their feelings. It's our attempt at active listening, and our intention is to make others not feel so alone. But in doing so, we've hijacked the thread. We've made it about us, not them.

You know you're doing this if you ever tell someone, "I know how you feel, because when this happened to me, [here's what I felt and did]..."

Here's a scenario to show you what this might look like in a work context.

Marketing executive Jacob (not his real name) once took on a job as VP of product marketing for a software company. He led the entire marketing function for this emerging enterprise and reported to the executive team. About a month into his tenure, without his knowledge, he found out they wanted to hire an SVP above him to run all of marketing. His ego bruised, he nonetheless accepted the decision—and it turned out to be one of the best partnerships of his career. The new exec became a lifelong mentor to him, and together they not only scaled the company, they brought it to a successful IPO.

Now a seasoned CMO in his own right, Jacob had a solid performer on his team, Alice, who had all the right skills to be an effective marketer, but the company needed a more experienced person to lead that team and scale for growth. The executive team made the decision to bring in someone

With engagement
falling, productivity
plummeting, and quiet
quitting rampant,
someone had to step
up to keep companies
moving forward.

above her. She was not happy with the decision. Jacob's intent was to bring the new leader in now and pave a career path for Alice as her skill set advanced. And his instinct was to address her concerns head-on by saying something like, "Alice, I know exactly how you feel. A few years ago, someone was brought in above me as a marketing leader, but my experience was..."

A fabulous intention to connect and show he understood how she felt, but it was not what Alice needed in that moment. She needed to be heard and understood. She needed the conversation to be about *her* concerns, *her* fears, and *her* path forward. If Jacob had plowed ahead with sharing his experiences first, that would've been empathy hijacking. And it would've eroded the trust between him and Alice.

The better choice that Jacob made was to sit down and talk with Alice, explain the business reasons and benefits of the decision, and give her space to air her concerns. He listened thoughtfully, taking notes and asking clarifying questions, and then offered, "It's a lot, isn't it? All your concerns are valid and I completely understand how you feel right now. I felt the same when a similar situation happened to me earlier in my career, and ultimately, we made a great team and it changed the trajectory of my career. Would you like to hear about that now, or would another time be better?" Alice made the decision to hear him out.

There's a time and place to share learnings from our experiences, but even when that time comes, we must do so only with explicit consent. I recommend saying something like, "Would it help if I shared something similar from my own experience?" The person you're speaking with may say yes or no, and you must respect their response. If you've laid the groundwork for truly robust two-way communication, they may say, "I just need to talk and be heard right now." Trust that they will approach you when they are ready for your advice.

Empathy hijacking is a misfire because it involves decentering the other person and inserting your own perspective, but it usually takes place in situations where empathy of *some* kind is an appropriate response. There are, however, some circumstances in which expressing empathy of *any* kind may feel wrong.

When Empathy Gets in the Way

Given my own work as an empathy advocate, it's no surprise that I believe empathy is critically important across most industries and use cases. But I don't believe empathy belongs everywhere at every moment.

Here's an example from my own life: in 2008, an undetected brain aneurysm ruptured and nearly killed me. The brain surgeon who saved my life was a very empathetic person when he spoke to my family outside the operating room. I appreciated that. However, I wouldn't want him crying over my suffering *while* he was performing surgery on me. In fact, I wouldn't want him distracted by my feelings or situation at all while he's operating! That's the time for focus and skill, *not* seeing, understanding, and feeling another person's perspective. A measure of cognitive empathy might be warranted, but emotional empathy could do more harm than good.

There are also times when leaders need to dial back their emotional empathy so they can steward the health of the overall business. Obviously, we want to show compassion for our employees as often as we can and across many scenarios—but not always at the expense of the company.

Chief marketing officer Tracy Eiler—who is also an author, speaker, highly empathetic leader in her own right, and one of the top fifteen most influential women in B2B marketing as named by Thomson Data—shared a story with me that underlined how even cognitive empathy needs to be tempered in certain situations. She said a colleague of hers had recently taken over management of a new team and wanted to bring everyone together for an in-person meeting. One of the colleague's team members pushed back.

"This person asked, 'Is it mandatory for me to travel to headquarters for this meeting? Because I have so much work to do. I just can't do it.' My friend was shocked. But she didn't waver; she went right to the heart of the issue, which on the surface appeared to be about workload. She asked, 'What is going on with your workload that you feel like you can't get on an airplane and come do what is obviously the right thing for the team and for the company?'"

Eiler went on to tell me that her friend opted *not* to express overt empathy during this conversation but instead reminded her team member that she was the new leader of the group and wanted him to be there for the in-person meeting. Since this gathering was going to be a tone-setting one where Eiler's friend would be establishing her leadership style, outlining goals, and assigning roles, she knew that all team members needed to participate in person. If Eiler's friend had believed that the wise and compassionate move was to let this team member sit out the meeting, she might have undermined herself as a new leader at the company and gotten the entire team off on the wrong foot. This was definitely a situation in which expectation-setting and realignment were more important than ensuring the employee could remain in his comfort zone.

Throughout this book, we'll explore other situations in which leaders must balance people needs with business needs. It's an issue that arises pretty frequently and one that must be handled with real care.

It's also considerably more common than situations in which leaders find themselves *actively attempting to apply empathy* in situations where it's not needed. They're more likely to do as Eiler's friend did and recognize when they need to put the business first for pragmatic reasons. Or they might try to handle tricky situations in non-empathetic ways, or they might misunderstand what empathy looks like in a work context. As we explored in Chapter 1, one of those common misunderstandings is believing that empathy only runs downhill, which can result in leaders taking on more and more duties themselves in the name of supporting their people.

Empathy ≠ Leaders Doing More Work Themselves

As I've mentioned, I've seen many, many leaders picking up the slack for their team members in the name of empathy. I spoke with Rebecca Friese, cofounder of workplace innovation consultancy FLYN, who said she's also seen an uptick in business leaders being asked to absorb the duties of their team members. And they do so for a variety of reasons.

"Just two years ago, we couldn't find enough talent to fill all these roles. Now we're experiencing hundreds and thousands of layoffs. So leaders are having to assume new roles and sometimes double, even triple the responsibility," she explained. "I had one executive client who was literally doing three roles at her company last year. Our advice was to talk with her team, but she told us, 'There's nobody else to do it. I either do it myself, or we fail.' This is not new for leaders, of course. They are constantly doing that dance, but it's been compounded in recent years."

As you might expect, much of this is due to fallout from the pandemic. Let's do a quick review of how employment and work changed during that challenging time.

In the spring of 2020—amid nationwide lockdowns, rampant COVID outbreaks, and global fear—20.5 million Americans were laid off from their jobs. In the months that followed, workers who remained on the payroll had to adjust to a new normal: working from home, nonstop video meetings, more work being done asynchronously, and other shifts. Some companies that had previously claimed remote work was an impossibility were forced to make it possible, and employees took note. By the second half of 2021, many workers felt quite differently about their work than they had just a few seasons previously. In the month of August 2021 alone, 4.3 million Americans quit their jobs. That marked the sixth consecutive month of record quitting rates according to the U.S. Bureau of Labor Statistics, a period that would eventually earn the title of the Great Resignation.

Meanwhile, the 7.7 million people who were unemployed at the time weren't exactly jumping at the roughly 10.4 million open positions on offer. Robert Reich, U.S. secretary of labor in the Clinton administration, commented on this phenomenon for *Time*, saying, "[Employees] don't want to return to backbreaking or boring, low wage, sh-t jobs. Workers are burned out. They're fed up. They're fried. In the wake of so much hardship, and illness and death during the past year, they're not going to take it anymore."

Something seismic was happening. And it wasn't over yet.

What followed was the now-famous phenomenon of quiet quitting: employees intentionally stopped going above and beyond, and instead they did what their job description required of them and only that. No more joining committees, no more organizing the team to buy birthday and baby shower gifts, no more office housework. People dialed back their commitments to any work that fell outside their assigned duties, and their employers panicked.

And no wonder. According to Gallup's *State of the Global Workplace* report for 2023, job dissatisfaction was at a staggering all-time high and only 23 percent of employees felt engaged at work. The report also found that these droves of unhappy, stressed workers were costing the global economy

$8.8 trillion in lost productivity. That's nearly 9 percent of the global GDP.

With engagement falling, productivity plummeting, and quiet quitting rampant, someone had to step up to keep companies moving forward. And in many cases, those "someones" were team leaders, managers, and executives.

Overtime hours, extra duties, and miscellaneous-but-mandatory tasks were once handled by team members but suddenly fell to their bosses. Some leaders felt like their own workloads doubled or tripled as they struggled to pick up the slack. And with people either quitting or quiet quitting, leaders also had to cope with nonstop efforts to replace their absent workers, along with reduced resources and increased pressure from their own supervisors.

"Because of all the shifts, leaders are being asked to take on so much more," said Friese. "Now they have to worry about the mental health of their employees. Now they must consider and be sensitive to how social and cultural forces, events, and changes are personally impacting employees' personal and professional lives, which inevitably and logically impacts their performance. On top of their regular work, leaders are being asked to take care of very personal things with their teams. Things that they are not equipped to do."

Sounds like a recipe for burnout, doesn't it?

The stress and pressures of additional duties and managing fears of their team members definitely took its toll on business leaders. Development Dimensions International's *Global Leadership Forecast 2021* polled thousands of business executives and HR professionals around the world, finding that nearly 60 percent felt used up at the end of the workday, a strong indicator of burnout.

Leadership strategist Kara Dennison wrote for *Forbes*, "Executives and leaders can be great decision-makers, but that doesn't necessarily mean they possess the skills to lead

Truly empathetic leaders understand their team members' logic and want to ensure everyone feels heard and valued, but they also know that business needs must be met.

people through times of personal and professional crises." She continued, "In addition, they often don't have the power or influence to change the culture and priorities of an organization to give their team members the compensation and respect they are demanding."

Maintaining empathy is hard enough under the best of working circumstances. It became incredibly challenging in the midst of overwhelm and burnout. And to make matters worse, a small subset of employees started turning business leaders' efforts at empathy against them.

Weaponized Empathy

Another unfortunate byproduct of the pandemic is a sense of entitlement among employees. Over the months and years following the 2020 COVID lockdowns, I began to hear more and more stories like these from business leaders.

- "I asked an employee to absorb a new task and they told me, 'You are not respecting my boundaries with that ask.'"

- "I needed him to do a few hours of overtime, something that was no big deal a few years ago, and he said, 'I will need to take some mental health days to process this.' I was stunned!"

- "We had a client emergency, but when I asked them to pitch in, they told me, 'You're not being very empathetic.'"

- "One of our employees claimed that the company was becoming less people-focused. They couldn't integrate their work and personal life because they couldn't get their errands or other personal activities done while working from nine to five!"

It came up so frequently that I eventually coined a term for this tactic: "weaponizing empathy." It happens when employees throw social and emotional words or phrases back at colleagues or managers to get what they want, taking advantage of their empathy. I want to emphasize that it's an infrequent phenomenon and one that often stems from legitimate concerns and questions. Please understand that I'm a huge supporter of giving people the right language to express themselves and their mental health needs. It's something I teach to and model with my own son. This should be celebrated and encouraged, given the world we live in. But when weaponized empathy does rear its head, things get ugly fast.

Here's how I believe this behavior pattern developed: workers from younger generations who had only been in the workforce a year or two when the pandemic hit have a skewed frame of reference. They may have had some experience with on-site work and rigid office rules, but they then spent nearly three years working remotely and doing so in an atmosphere of extreme, near-universal flexibility. This meant that their view of the modern workplace was far different from past generations.

These workers got used to having their preferences met and their employers bend over backwards to accommodate their schedules. Many companies made employee mental health a priority at the start of the pandemic, instructing leaders to do whatever necessary to help overwhelmed employees cope. This was especially important in the tight labor market.

Then when the state of emergency finally began to ebb and companies asked people to return to the office, some of these workers were confused and aggravated. They'd been able to do their work, participate, and innovate from home. They hadn't gotten pushback or been assigned extra duties in *literal years*. Why was this shift necessary? Couldn't they just continue prioritizing work as they saw fit or work from home indefinitely or refuse to execute tasks that felt joyless and draining? To them, it seemed like a forced rewind: a return to older, worse, more stressful, and less rewarding times. And that felt untenable.

Another subset of employees may not have been younger people but people with a sharp eye for loopholes. They, too, saw that the return to on-site work, occasional overtime, and rigid working hours could be pushed against. Their managers had been so accommodating and flexible for so long, and that felt great. Now they could use that precedent to insist that turning back the clock was illogical and unreasonable.

They could use the empathy they'd been recently shown as leverage for meeting their present-day demands. Even if those demands were—in some instances, not all—unreasonable.

In some cases, empathy gets weaponized simply because employees are unhappy with new protocols or restrictions. An executive at a software company told me that his firm once had an unlimited vacation policy, something they created to help their employees rest and recoup as well as feel valued by leadership. But when multiple people began taking three weeks off every single quarter, the company had to create some guardrails. The policy had been based on an expectation that people wouldn't take advantage. When some in the workforce proved themselves inconsiderate, the policy was altered to protect the business. Company employees were outraged by this and accused management of moving away from being people-centric. An accusation like that cut to the core of the leadership team, especially since they had originally designed these policies to put people first.

It doesn't help that books like *The 4-Hour Workweek* and *The Five-Hour Workday* circulate ideas about productivity that don't apply to most workers and workplaces. Or that there is a flood of articles encouraging people to demand more, stick to their guns, and never do work that dulls their shine. For example, in early 2023, *Girlboss* emailed its readers and encouraged them to create a "to-don't list" to help identify pain points in their current work roles.

> Think about the things you hate doing in your day-to-day. Do you dread one-on-ones with your boss? Do you shudder each time you open an Excel sheet? Jot it down! Identifying these small details could help you understand where things are going wrong—i.e., whether you're stuck in an ill-fitting company culture or a simple routine rut.

To be crystal clear, I don't believe people should grind themselves down to nubs doing work they loathe. I also don't believe innovative and collaborative work can only happen inside a four-walled office. I believe honoring mental health, compassionate accommodation, and human understanding should be the norm in every single organization and that many of the issues mentioned above could be remedied with clear communication (the Clarity Pillar we'll talk about later). Like all successful business leaders, I know that the best way to keep employees motivated, engaged, happy, and productive is to ensure they focus on tasks they enjoy doing and can excel at. I also believe that people-centric companies that treat their employees well, respect them, and offer them real flexibility are the best places to work. My perception of weaponized empathy, however, is that some outliers have found ways to capitalize on a shift in work philosophy and milk it to their advantage. And those outliers are poisoning the well for everyone else.

Weaponized empathy can cause agony for truly empathetic business leaders. They understand their team members' logic and want to ensure everyone feels heard and valued, but they also know that business needs must be met. They have their own higher-ups to answer to, and if those higher-ups insist that everyone needs to get back to their cubicles, they are expected to make that happen.

If leaders ignore
the Five Pillars,
they run the risk
of being bulldozed
and manipulated.

Unfortunately, weaponized empathy will continue to show up if leaders lack the strength or resolve to create and communicate new boundaries. If leaders ignore the Five Pillars, they run the risk of being bulldozed and manipulated.

As you'll see in later chapters, leaders who embrace the Five Pillars are the ones who are best equipped to navigate any and all empathy-related challenges.

Layoffs Led with Compassion

Let's circle back to layoffs, an activity that nearly every leader dreads. Now that we've seen all the ways our attempts at empathetic leadership can backfire, I want to reassure you that even the most stressful, emotionally fraught, diplomatically tricky situations *can and should* be handled with empathy.

While working as COO at a software company, business builder and senior technology executive Dave Zinman (whom you met earlier) was asked to help pivot the business away from one of its two core competencies. It was a decision that made strategic sense, but it meant Zinman would have to facilitate some pretty serious layoffs.

He told me about how he handled this, saying,

> We tried to do it with real empathy. For instance, as soon as we made the decision and knew how long the pivot might take, we told everybody. We said, "This is what's happening. This is the strategy. We don't think we're going to execute this for another two months, it's going to take us time, but we want to let everybody know now so you can all decide on your next steps." We gave people as much notice as we could. We wanted to avoid springing it on them and saying, "Sorry, but today's your last day."

This is a perfect example of using the Decisiveness Pillar to share critical information as soon as possible! Zinman's layoff communication strategy also invoked the Clarity Pillar, since he and his team also explained why the pivot made sense for the company on a strategic level. He made sure that each person understood there was a business-critical reason they were being laid off. They wouldn't be happy about it, but at least they would have a logical explanation.

Zinman's empathy extended to the employees who remained on the payroll of this company too. He knew that people who are not eliminated during layoffs are called "survivors" for a good reason.

"All of that work, that communication, helped a lot. After those people were gone, the people that were left had to refocus on the new business direction. And I knew they'd be looking around at the empty chairs surrounding them. Layoffs are a traumatic event. I wanted the team members who remained to see that we'd treated the people that were leaving really well, that we explained everything, and that anyone who was laid off understood why the company was heading in the direction it was heading."

I have experienced Zinman's compassionate layoff process myself because he was once my own boss! He was tasked with laying off the entire marketing team in advance of a company merger. Much as we disliked being let go, he supported us, broke the news gently, gave real thought ahead of time to address our concerns or questions, and even provided job leads and references to set us on a new path. Zinman truly sat with us with encouragement and support for as much time as we needed as we processed this unpleasant surprise (rather than sending us a cold, impersonal email), and it made a huge difference in how we felt during and after we were told our time with the company had ended. This is why I often say that one of my most empathetic bosses actually had to lay me off! And that's why I still value him as a mentor and trusted colleague to this very day.

Now I understand that some companies have had to lay off workers at such scale and in dispersed environments due to either remote work or pandemic health guidelines, but leaving out a personal and human touch is just wrong. And not allowing managers to reach out with a comforting phone call or reply to panicked texts in order to protect the company for legal reasons (as was the case with several mass tech company layoffs in the last few years) is simply inhumane.

Sadly, Zinman's executive team at that software company mentioned at the beginning of this section may currently be the exception, not the rule. Many leaders who aim for empathy end up missing the mark because we misunderstand when and how to express it, because we conflate empathy with people-pleasing or doing more work ourselves, or because our compassion gets turned against us by our team members. We try to make empathetic choices but end up going wrong for so many reasons.

We also go wrong because of who we are and what we've experienced, as we'll see in the next chapter. Different paradigms and expectations can make it challenging to see the perspectives of our colleagues and use that information to act compassionately.

Chapter Highlights

- Empathy hijacking occurs when people unintentionally shift the focus to themselves by immediately sharing their own related stories; despite good intent, this inadvertently undermines genuine connection.

- In some cases, leaders must carefully balance empathy with business needs, recognizing that there are situations where prioritizing empathy may not be in the company's best interest.

- Some leaders mistakenly believe that empathy entails people-pleasing or taking on additional work themselves, potentially leading to burnout and reduced effectiveness.

- Weaponized empathy, where employees cite a lack of empathy to challenge policies or seek preferential treatment, can complicate leaders' efforts to strike a balance between empathy and business priorities.

- Effective communication, clarity, and compassion, especially in challenging situations like layoffs, play a crucial role in maintaining trust and ensuring that employees comprehend the reasons behind significant decisions.

GENERATIONAL CLASHES AND OTHER COMPLICATING FACTORS

Difference Is Powerful—If You Know How to Navigate It

"We will all profit from a more diverse, inclusive society, understanding, accommodating, even celebrating our differences, while pulling together for the common good."
RUTH BADER GINSBURG, associate justice of the U.S. Supreme Court

LET'S START by addressing the proverbial elephant in the room: generational issues are touchy.

Whether you're a member of Gen Z (born 1997–2010) or a baby boomer (born 1946–1964), a Gen Xer (born 1965–1980) or a millennial (born 1981–1996), you're likely sick to death of the assumptions and stereotypes associated with your age group. And no wonder, since many of them are overblown or just plain wrong. Even if they make hilarious memes!

But there's no denying that different generations can hold different views and values. Even when they don't truly differ that much, *our belief* that they differ can impact our reactions, according to social and industrial-organizational psychologists. We make assumptions or accusations and, in doing so, influence our office dynamics. It happens frequently enough that age-group clashes in the workplace have become an unavoidable trope, and one that can be corrosive to leaders' attempts at empathy.

Other elements of personal identity like ability, gender identity, sexual orientation, religion, belonging to an underrepresented or marginalized group, body size, and native language also impact the ways that leaders and team members interact. The fact that we live in a diverse world is undeniably good, but it means we don't always share or understand the life experiences of our colleagues.

As we continue to explore the reasons that workplace empathy feels so dang hard, we need to undertake careful—and respectful—examination of how interpersonal and identity differences add a layer of complexity.

Why Older Employees Distrust Their Employers

One thing that sets boomers apart from other generations is that many of them lived through the shift to shareholder value. Let's take a quick spin through recent economic history to get some context.

There was a time when companies looked after their people. Yes, really! During the 1950s and '60s, the U.S. economy was flourishing. Postwar conditions, an emerging middle class, and diversification of jobs all fed into a market that was, well, booming. And though it may seem implausible now, the large corporations of that period felt they had enough wealth to spread around; they paid their workers robust wages, set up pension funds for retired employees, gave out bonuses, and still had plenty left over to keep shareholders happy. This is why some people stayed with a single employer for their entire careers. They were loyal because their companies actually took care of them. The people who lived through this era were parents to the baby boomer generation. That means many boomers witnessed their families achieve success and accumulate wealth in an America where workers were relentlessly faithful to their employers.

But then came the shake-up.

In 1976, economists Michael C. Jensen and William H. Meckling published an incendiary paper titled "Theory of the Firm: Managerial Behavior, Agency Costs and Ownership Structure" in the *Journal of Financial Economics*. In it, they claimed that all corporations built to reward employees and serve customers were destroying the U.S. economy. They insisted that these organizations were shirking their responsibility to produce returns for their shareholders. When shareholders got wind of this, they started making noise.

Once-satisfied shareholders suddenly began complaining to companies that their returns were pitifully low, leveraging Jensen and Meckling's assertions as proof. In short order, business leaders realized that they'd better "maximize shareholder value" or risk losing their jobs. In just a few years, executives started acting as if they worked for their shareholders and no one else. By the dawn of the 1980s, corporate boards were focused on getting company leadership and shareholder interests aligned, often by tempting their executives with stock-based bonuses. In *New to Big*, David Kidder and Christina Wallace summarize this phenomenon beautifully, writing:

> There were no laws in place that forced executives to fulfill shareholders' fiduciary expectations. Executives pledged allegiance to the corporation itself, and were expected to act in its best interests. Shareholders were contractually entitled to the "residual value" of the corporation after its other financial obligations had been fulfilled, but nowhere did any doctrine state that corporate leadership must actively work to boost that residual value. This was not an encoded shift, but instead a tacit agreement among CEOs and investors. And one that persists to this day.

Companies went from an abundance mindset to a constant scramble for profits. Layoffs, downsizing, mergers, and recessions followed while employees everywhere became second-class citizens. Many of those employees were boomers. And many of them grew to distrust the companies they worked for after living through this sea change.

Since members of this generation are now in leadership roles within businesses across the globe, it's no wonder so many employees have come to view their employers as "the man," "big brother," an entity that wants to squeeze the most out of them while rewarding them with the bare minimum. Boomers watched their parents earn handsomely at stable jobs, but by the time they came of age, no such generosity or stability could be found. They felt betrayed and jilted. This causes some of them to create distance with others at work, put up walls, and hoard information for their own survival.

And now other generations have joined the leadership ranks so things get further complicated. Gen X grew up as fiercely independent: one of the first generations of latchkey kids, who often get right down to business to solve problems on their own. Millennials grew up as digital natives and social media users, so they are more technologically savvy and used to having a voice in everything. They see shared information as power to solve problems. Growing up in an age of constant data and entertainment, they can get bored more easily and enjoy taking on different roles and challenges.

And here's where it all combusts: according to the Bureau of Labor Statistics, as of 2023, there are five generations in the workplace: traditionalists, baby boomers, Generation X, millennials, and Generation Z. These categories cover everyone from teenagers to octogenarians.

All these generations in the workplace think a certain way, and sometimes expect their teams to see the world—and the work—in the same way they do. And when that is not intentionally understood, therein lies the rub.

The Era of Empathy

Fast-forward several decades, and the tide was shifting again. By the 2010s, we had just come out of a nerve-racking financial crisis caused by the 2008 housing market collapse that led into stimulus programs and new regulations. Things were tough for college grads but a boon for those already in the workforce. Unemployment was low, a record number of jobs were created, more women were in the workforce than ever before, and pay rates rose. As economic conditions improved, so did conditions for workers. Distributed teams, remote work, and flexible schedules became more common.

And empathy—along with annoyingly titled "soft skills" under the umbrella of emotional intelligence—was being prioritized both formally and informally. A flood of research proved that empathetic workplaces are more likely to foster stronger collaboration, cause less stress for their employees, and enjoy higher levels of morale. Employees working for empathetic companies even bounce back more quickly from career hiccups and challenges, including the dreaded lay-offs. By 2017, 20 percent of U.S. employers offered empathy training for their managers, and a 2019 survey of 150 CEOs reported that more than 80 percent saw empathy as key to business success.

Jon Shanahan, president and CEO of Businessolver, a leader in SaaS-based benefits technology and services that puts out an annual *State of Workplace Empathy* report, told *Forbes* in 2021, "After years of decline, workplace empathy has improved—alongside overall attentiveness to issues long considered to be among the most difficult to discuss in the workplace, including our lives outside of work, mental health, and race."

And then? COVID.

As we learned in Chapter 2, the pandemic initially brought a surge of additional empathy to workplaces, but once lockdowns lifted and companies attempted to get "back to normal," trouble arose. Flexibility was reined in, work-from-home privileges revoked, and workers were asked to shift their priorities to align with company goals. Leaders felt they were doing what was best for their businesses, but employees felt deprioritized. It almost seemed as if many leaders who begrudgingly leaned in to flexibility for survival said, "You've had your fun. Now it's time to get back to the grind." In an article for *Business Insider*, journalist Rebecca Knight wrote, "Workers, especially younger ones, grew accustomed to this warmer, gentler management style, and amid a tight labor market, it became an expectation." Once that warmer, gentler management style began to fade away, those younger workers rebelled. Millennials and Gen Z employees started feeling how their boomer colleagues felt decades ago: betrayed and jilted.

"There are workplace circumstances that baby boomers dreamed about like work-life balance, having a boss who was kind, and job security. But those things were just a dream for them because there were eighty million of them competing with each other," said generational expert, consultant, and keynote speaker Anna Liotta, author of the book *Unlocking Generational CODES*. In an interview for *The Empathy Edge* podcast, she told me, "Gen Xers desired many of the same things, but there were fewer of them, and they had less leverage to apply. By the time millennials arrived, they were making actual demands. So boomers dreamed it, Gen Xers desired it, millennials demanded it, and now Gen Z knows they deserve it."

As we've explored, these demographic shifts led to wonderful things such as opening up conversations about mental health, more flexible schedules and benefits, and a greater focus on integrating personal and work life. But as with any good thing, too much can have drawbacks. Sometimes these experiences and feelings can lead to manipulation of employer empathy, as we discussed earlier when talking about empathy hijacking. They can also lead to quiet quitting, diminished productivity, and interpersonal strife as well as slightly less disruptive issues, with no less harmful impacts to the company's bottom line, like employee dissatisfaction or disengagement. However they manifest, they create tension.

In addition to generational differences and clashes, there are some issues specific to certain populations that can surface and stretch empathy-related challenges.

Group-Specific Factors

There are more identities, ethnic groups, and subpopulations than I can possibly list here, so it will be equally impossible for me (or anyone) to comprehensively summarize their workplace experiences. But I do want to touch upon some non-generational factors that seem to pop up regularly across industries. I'd encourage you to explore beyond this section to learn about others that might affect your industry or organization. I also want to point out two key concepts before moving forward:

1   **Our differences are challenging but also enriching.** The people who work with us have a wide range of life experiences, views, biases, and perspectives. Although these differences can sometimes cause friction, they should never be targeted for eradication. Diversity is a strength that brings innovation, insight, and creativity to every company. According to *Forbes*, "Companies with above-average diversity produced a greater proportion of revenue from innovation (45 percent of total) than from companies with below average diversity (26 percent). This 19 percent innovation-related advantage translated into overall better financial performance."

2   **Understanding leads to empathy.** Acknowledging that people come from diverse backgrounds and bring different things to the table allows us to access even more

Millennials and Gen Z employees started feeling how their boomer colleagues felt decades ago: betrayed and jilted.

empathy. Learning about how our unique life experiences lead to different perspectives enables us to understand each other, uncover new solutions, and collaborate more effectively.

So, all that said, let's examine a few examples of groups who face empathy challenges.

First-Generation Professionals (FGPs)

Michelle Hoover, founder of Baem Leadership, defines FGPs as being among the first persons in their immediate family to obtain a college degree or to be hired for a higher-level professional position than was held by either parent. This group often includes people raised in rural areas and individuals from working-class backgrounds. FGP workers have a reputation for being incredibly resilient and hard-working, but they also enter the workforce at a disadvantage. They may be trailblazers in their own families, but at work they sometimes lack insider knowledge and context for office politics and social mores, which can cause interpersonal friction and misunderstandings. FGPs may also struggle to understand how to advance their careers or move up in the ranks, and they can benefit from mentoring and support from leaders.

Underrepresented and Marginalized Ethnic Identities

Entire books have been written about the challenges that people with underrepresented and marginalized ethnic identities face at work. Black and Brown people, immigrants, Indigenous people, members of religious minorities, and other groups who share common cultural backgrounds or descent often face resistance, misunderstanding, microaggressions, unconscious bias, and even outright discrimination in their workplaces. It's the responsibility of leaders to cultivate understanding of these challenges and develop empathetic strategies that respect people's differences.

Underrepresented and Marginalized
Gender or Sexual Identities

As diversity has become celebrated and encouraged in many workplaces, this new dialogue also exposes misunderstanding and prejudice from those who are not willing or able to understand.

Empathy tensions may affect queer, gay, lesbian, transgender, gender fluid, asexual, or bisexual people in the workplace, especially with coworkers from older generations. Gender and sexual identity expression was suppressed for decades, so many baby boomers express discomfort with these identities "suddenly" appearing in their workplaces (even though LGBTQ+ colleagues have always been here but were forced into silence). It's also important to note that there are many subcultures and differences within this catch-all category; it is not just one homogenous group. Again, leadership must take the helm to facilitate understanding, acceptance, and empathy.

People with Differing Abilities

People who have physical differences, neurodiverse people, and people who struggle with mental health challenges may have long-standing workplace regulations in their favor, but they still come up against coworker bias and misunderstanding. This is especially true if these workers need extra accommodations, resources, and time to complete certain tasks; if they communicate or process information differently; or if they have a disability that is invisible to observers. It's worth noting that most people with differing abilities welcome empathy in their workplaces but tend to rankle at sympathy or pity. "Good for them"-type sentiments feel condescending and othering, so they must be avoided.

Tiffany Dufu is the founder of The Cru, a company that facilitates women's peer-coaching and accountability circles to help them meet their life goals. (The Cru was acquired by

Luminary in 2023.) When I interviewed her for my podcast, I asked her to share the best ways to connect with people across diverse experiences and backgrounds. She revealed three principles that help her keep her own teams and projects aligned with and empathetic toward each other:

> First is having some kind of **organizing principle**, a foundation for why it is you're coming together. For us at The Cru, it's intentions. We're here to help one another realize our life intentions and that is the core purpose of our gathering. We all share that common mission of supporting one another in identifying our life intentions.
>
> Second is to **set norms to set expectations**. What does effective communication mean to you? What does commitment mean to you? Really identify the behaviors that people are going to agree upon.
>
> Third is having **a very clear mechanism for how you'll interact with one another**. This provides some much-needed structure so everyone is on the same page. At The Cru, that mechanism is the actual gathering of participants. We also have mechanisms for how we interact at these gatherings: people take turns, there's a timekeeper, there's a notetaker, people share, they receive a series of open-ended questions from their colleagues.
>
> All three of these help people from a variety of backgrounds level-set expectations with each other.

Dufu is absolutely spot-on with these recommendations. Setting expectations and laying down ground rules can help people who might otherwise clash to feel comfortable collaborating. Even when those people come from incredibly different backgrounds, hold differing generational viewpoints, or have diverse life experiences.

Another fantastic resource for any business leader hoping to navigate relationships with workers from any of the groups we've discussed in this chapter is Karen Catlin's book

Better Allies. Catlin is a leadership coach and speaker on inclusive workplaces, and her book offers both real-world examples of tough situations and actionable tactics for navigating them in your own workplace.

See the Further Reading section at the end of this book to dive deeper into many of the concepts and tactics found throughout.

So, What's Next?

This entire section of the book has been dedicated to exploring why empathy in workplaces can seem so hard. The main reason, of course, is that there's a lot to consider and navigate, especially as social and interpersonal dynamics continue to evolve. Workplaces are made up of humans, and we humans are not easy creatures, especially when we interact with each other! We talked about the dangers of well-intentioned empathy hijacking, how easy it can be for leaders to absorb extra work or avoid conflict to keep everyone happy, the weaponized empathy phenomenon, and all the ways our unique life experiences can make empathy challenging. Hopefully, you feel seen and validated after reading about how these dilemmas are affecting business leaders everywhere.

You're not alone. Leaders—and even aspiring leaders—like you who have embraced compassionate leadership are struggling with some very hard challenges around setting boundaries, achieving high performance, and avoiding burnout, among others.

And you're not wrong to continually champion compassion! Research shows that not only is empathy in leadership and culture good for the bottom line, it's what the incoming generations are demanding. Companies that give up on building people-centric cultures are slamming the door in the face of everything that millennials, Gen Zers, and all the future people they need to hire are seeking in a modern workplace: flexibility, camaraderie, the ability to make an impact, authenticity, professional development, mentorship, project ownership, a variety of challenges, and advancement potential, to name a few.

As we move on to Part II, we'll start investigating strategies, mindset shifts, and solutions. The second half of this book is all about helping you remain an *effectively* empathetic and compassionate leader without losing yourself in the process.

I promise it can be done! And the Five Pillars of Effective Empathetic Leadership are critical to making it possible. So in Part II, let's explore each pillar in depth and uncover the related principles and tactics that will support you in your empathetic leadership journey.

Chapter Highlights

- With five generations all working together in one workplace, generational mindset and expectation differences are complex and often involve assumptions and stereotypes that can affect office dynamics. These differences can impact how leaders and team members interact, communicate, and perform, and they require careful examination.

- The shift to shareholder value in the corporate world in the 1980s led to a significant change in how companies operated. Loyalty to employees waned, leading to distrust among older generations, particularly baby boomers, who had seen their parents experience a different model of corporate loyalty.

- The era of empathy in the workplace emerged in the 2010s, with a focus on fostering collaboration, reducing stress, and improving morale. Empathy was seen as crucial to business success, with many companies offering empathy training for managers.

- The COVID-19 pandemic initially brought increased empathy to workplaces, but as companies returned to pre-pandemic norms, employees, particularly millennials and Gen Zers, felt deprioritized, leading to tensions and feelings of betrayal.

- Workplace empathy challenges go beyond generational differences and also include issues related to first-generation professionals, underrepresented and marginalized ethnic identities, underrepresented and marginalized gender or sexual identities, and people with differing abilities. It's essential for leaders to cultivate understanding and empathy in these diverse contexts, so everyone can do their best work.

THE FIVE PILLARS OF EFFECTIVE EMPATHETIC LEADERSHIP

SELF-AWARENESS

I Might Be the Problem.
And That's Okay!

"Self-awareness is one of the most important things a leader can cultivate. Before you can lead others, you have to have a great awareness of your values."
RHONDA GEORGE-DENNISTON, chief learning and development officer at TBWA\Worldwide

What Is Self-Awareness? Understanding your own strengths, blind spots, emotions, leadership style, and triggers. And helping your team members understand theirs.

Why Is Self-Awareness Important? Self-awareness helps you to understand complaints and constructive feedback, know when you might need help navigating a situation, and take accountability for your actions. Also it helps you know where you shine and where you can best contribute and complement your team.

NOW, YOU might be saying to yourself, "Hang on, Maria. Isn't it more important for me to understand my team members? Do I really have to do a bunch of woo-woo self-reflection?"

And my answer is this: *both* are crucial. And self-reflection is not woo-woo; it's smart strategy. You need to cultivate a deep and ever-evolving understanding of your people, as well as of yourself. Here's a real-life story that proves this knowledge can be a game-changer.

John Kreisa is chief marketing officer at Couchbase where all employees are encouraged to embrace the Enneagram test. This test is one of several trusted personality evaluations that helps people understand their strengths, challenges, problem-solving strategies, and interpersonal dynamics. Kreisa shared that Couchbase CEO Matt Cain is a huge fan of the test in professional settings—someone who can list all nine Enneagram types and their characteristics off the cuff—and his enthusiasm has permeated the company culture.

"I'm an Enneagram nine, the Peacemaker, which helps me recognize that I'm somewhat conflict averse... but not so much that I can't initiate tough conversations," said Kreisa. "All my leaders have taken the test too. And knowing that this person is an eight and that person is a two helps me understand their drivers."

Kreisa believes this combination of self-knowledge and knowledge of his team members helps him be a better, more empathetic leader. It enables him to see and understand why the people around him react in certain ways. He's even encountered situations in which Enneagram types have helped him process situations retroactively.

"Recently I was trying to convince one employee to move from his current department over to my department," he said. "Even though I felt I was presenting him with a no-brainer by asking him to run this project for me, I had to call him four times, including twice over the weekend, to convince him! When I mentioned this to our CEO, he said, 'That totally makes sense to me based on his Enneagram type. I'm not surprised at all he's looking at it this way, but I bet he gets there eventually.' And sure enough, he did. Understanding the personality types helps me avoid getting frustrated with myself and others."

Clearly, Kreisa, his team, and his company have learned the value of self-awareness, but other leaders and companies lag behind. In fact, one reason I've made self-awareness the first Pillar of Effective Empathetic Leadership is that many leaders don't immediately recognize its value. Despite it being something of a buzzword in management circles, self-awareness can seem like a low priority, especially for leaders who are constantly putting out fires and juggling crises. Who has time to navel-gaze when there are deadlines to hit and shareholder demands to be met? Plus business leadership can feel like an externalized activity, one in which you spend time coaching and directing *others*, instead of looking inward.

But study after study has shown that when leaders embrace self-reflection, they actually become more effective at their jobs. One such study featured in the *MIT Sloan Management Review* summarized more than two thousand in-depth conversations with international executives and stated that the most successful leaders understand where their natural inclinations lie and use this insight to either augment those inclinations or redirect them. Clearly, leaders who take the time to get to know themselves and adjust accordingly are the ones getting the best results.

On top of that helpful insight, organizational psychologist Dr. Tasha Eurich wrote in *Harvard Business Review* that "when we see ourselves clearly, we are more confident and more creative. We make sounder decisions, build stronger relationships, and communicate more effectively. We're less likely to lie, cheat, and steal. We are better workers who get more promotions. And we're more-effective leaders with more-satisfied employees." Quite the laundry list of reasons to cultivate self-knowledge!

And that's not all. Self-aware leaders help drive better financial performance. Yet another study, run by Korn Ferry International, surveyed 486 publicly traded companies and found that those with strong financial performance had employees with higher levels of self-awareness than poorly performing companies.

Pretty compelling evidence, right? And it all makes sense. A conscious understanding of your motives, personality, and behaviors—including how these things affect your leadership style—positions you to maximize your strengths and course-correct around your weaknesses. Without that awareness, it's much harder to make sound business decisions. And *considerably* harder to be an empathetic leader of people.

Contrary to its false reputation as a weakness, empathy requires great strength. You must get your own house in order, so to speak, to take in the perspectives of others without fear or defensiveness. If you don't truly understand your own reactions or triggers—if you can't stand firm in who you are and how you operate—you'll struggle to connect with team members. You might even start to find their innovative ideas threatening and stop listening to them.

Now here's the contradiction: some of the most valuable self-awareness stems from *external* feedback.

That's right: in order to truly know yourself you need to *hear and heed* the things your colleagues tell you. Undoubtedly, you can identify a few of your own talents and challenges, but the process of cultivating deep and ever-evolving self-knowledge is one that requires outside input.

Don't be scared. You'll be fine. In fact, letting go of your ego and being curious enough to learn and grow is a sure sign that you are truly tapping into your empathy.

Here's a great story from that MIT study I mentioned above:

> In an article in *Fortune International*, Lauren Zalaznick, now chairman, Entertainment & Digital Networks and Integrated Media for NBCUniversal, recalled that the best advice she ever received was from her first boss, who told her: "Throughout your career, you're going to hear lots of feedback from show-makers and peers and employees and bosses. If you hear a certain piece of feedback consistently and you don't agree with it, it doesn't matter what you think. Truth is, you're being perceived that way."

This may not be the news that many business leaders want to hear, but it's news they need to accept. If you're working hard to be a diplomatic communicator but still getting the input that you seem brusque and curt, that's worth examining. If you believe you're a stellar listener but people tell you they never feel heard, embrace that feedback. Your team is not clear on the instructions you gave? You can say you explained it in detail one hundred times, but if they don't understand, that's on you. Self-awareness isn't only about what you understand about yourself; it's also about how your motives, personality, and behaviors are seen by those around you.

It's not enough to defend your *intentions*. It's about the *actual impact* you have. I like to define the difference between intention and impact this way: if I accidentally trip you, causing you to land on your face and break your nose, no matter how much I didn't intend to do it, that doesn't make the impact any less painful. And so that pain should be acknowledged.

So how does this pillar support leaders who specifically and mindfully embrace compassionate practice?

Let's find out.

How Does Self-Awareness Benefit Empathetic Leaders?

Cultivating this pillar will help you become a better leader (and, frankly, human) overall, but it will be especially helpful if you want to lead empathetically without burning yourself out. Here's how.

Your Character Impacts Your Interactions with Team Members

When you talk with your colleagues and subordinates, are you aware of how your communication style and personality affect them? Do they find you intimidating, condescending, or inattentive? If you don't know, how can you expect them to be honest and authentic with you? And further, how can you change your behaviors, so they know how much you care? Good intentions are wonderful, but at the end of the day, it's impact that matters.

On the flip side, your character may be overly accommodating or pliable, and team members may learn to take advantage of that. If you lack awareness, you won't be able to set the boundaries you need to shield yourself from bad actors. (Something we'll explore more when we talk about self-care in Chapter 5.)

Understanding Yourself as a Leader Builds Trust

Employees feel comfortable putting their trust in leaders who hold themselves accountable. People instinctively respect leaders who are honest about their leadership styles and shortcomings. You can admit you're wrong, unsure, or not as good at something as your team so they can understand where they complement you. By knowing yourself, you will create an environment where team members feel confident relying on you.

Self-Awareness Keeps You Open to Change

Empathetic leaders don't just listen and respond; they also adjust their behaviors when they realize that doing so will be beneficial. An up-to-date understanding of your emotions, leadership style, and triggers helps you remain open to making some changes in your reactions. This can mean being more lenient and receptive but can also mean learning to say no more frequently or training yourself to become more decisive. Self-awareness also allows you to vary your leadership style to suit specific situations and personality types, a certain flexibility that many empathetic leaders exhibit.

You'll Champion Learning and Development

Self-aware leaders tend to promote advancement in the people they supervise. They become strong role models. When your team members see that you're aware of—and working

Contrary to its
false reputation
as a weakness,
empathy requires
great strength.

to refine—your own strengths and weaknesses, they will feel encouraged to do the same. And when you see yourself as being on a journey of self-awareness, you're more likely to support and mentor those around you.

Speaking of being on a journey, self-awareness is something that the best leaders cultivate on an ongoing basis throughout their careers. So if you worry you're not as cognizant of your motives, personality, and behaviors as you could be, don't sweat it. Read on to find out how you can continually fortify this pillar every single day.

How to Become More Self-Aware

You might be surprised to hear that practicing introspection doesn't always lead to bolstered self-awareness. In her study in the *Harvard Business Review*, Dr. Eurich found that people who introspect are actually *less* self-aware and report worse job satisfaction and well-being! She asserts this is because probing our own thoughts and behaviors doesn't enable us to dive deep enough.

"Research has shown that we simply do not have access to many of the unconscious thoughts, feelings, and motives we're searching for," she wrote. "And because so much is trapped outside of our conscious awareness, we tend to invent answers that *feel* true but are often wrong."

So what should you try instead?

Request Input from Team Members and Colleagues

Since you won't be able to surface all of your blind spots—traits or beliefs that impact how you behave, what you believe, and how effective you can be—you'll need help. Challenging as it may feel, the best way to see these blind spots clearly is to ask for feedback from the people around you. This includes leadership colleagues, who can give you input at the peer level, and team members, who can tell you what it's like to have you as a boss. Both types of feedback are valuable in different ways, so it's best to ensure you get a little of each.

And getting both types will require you to actively ask for them.

"You really have to ask for feedback," said Rhonda George-Denniston, chief learning and development officer at TBWA\ Worldwide, "which means you need to have great relationships with your people so you can *ask* for that feedback. It's difficult getting feedback from the people who are reporting to you, but doing so will truly expand your self-awareness. Make it part of your growth strategy to seek feedback from others."

Here are some tactics to try:

- **Create an anonymous suggestion box:** Yes, I know it's not exactly a leading-edge tactic, but it's helped facilitate gathering sensitive input for *centuries*! If your business unit or department doesn't currently have a culture of open feedback, people may need to ease into it. As a starting point, you can set up an anonymous suggestion box (physical or digital) specific to your own performance. How do others feel things are going? What could use improvement? Ask them to drop you a note or chime in on a feedback-specific Slack channel whenever they notice something in your leadership style that's especially challenging or supportive.

- **Ask for input at regular intervals:** Once your team members and colleagues are accustomed to providing performance feedback, incorporate requests into any regular meetings. These can be weekly one-on-ones or quarterly check-ins with your most trusted employees and colleagues. Perhaps ask the question in every one-to-one, "What can I be doing better to empower you?"

- **Institute 360 reviews:** Consider requesting feedback from colleagues, supervisors, and subordinates through a 360-degree feedback process. This way, you can assess how you are doing as a leader but also how colleagues, direct reports, and your own boss view your performance.

- **Assemble a personal advisory board:** Advisory boards aren't just for businesses! As a leader, you can create your own peer support group, mastermind group, or peer-to-peer coaching circle to help you see and overcome challenges. This can be a formal group or an ad hoc, casual one with trusted peers that meets regularly. You'll benefit as a leader, and if you allow feedback to flow both ways this type of group can serve as a reality check for all members. You'll come together to support each other's growth and development, get unbiased feedback in a safe place, share experiences, seek advice, and gain perspective. Almost all the strong and successful empathetic leaders I've researched participate in a group like this.

Spoiler alert: in the next pillar, Self-Care, you'll discover how to build emotional regulation to constructively take in all this feedback without defensiveness or fear.

Leverage Self-Assessment Tools

There are hundreds of tests, diagnostics, and self-assessment tools out there that can help leaders get clarity on their leadership style, strengths, challenges, and triggers. None is foolproof, but all will help you fine-tune your understanding of yourself as a leader.

Brandon Miller is constantly preaching the gospel of self-assessment tools. An author, certified strengths coach, and CEO of coaching and consulting firm 34 Strong, he has seen these tests help leaders understand how to maximize their strengths and navigate tough situations with empathy.

"I think any psychometric assessment that is effective gives us the gift of self-awareness," Miller explained. "I get to know who I am. I get to know who I'm not. I get to know myself in my best place, my worst place, and everything in the middle. And if I can get to the point where I can know myself that way without judgment, I have climbed the ladder of emotional intelligence. I am now able to look at myself objectively, which allows me to then look at you in that way as well."

Here are some tactics to try:

- **Myers-Briggs® Type Indicator (MBTI):** This long-trusted tool helps you see how you leverage perception and judgment as you move through the world. By answering a series of questions, the MBTI tool sorts you into one of sixteen personality types and then offers you a high-level overview of how your type typically operates. By highlighting which behaviors come naturally and which ones don't, this tool helps you understand which elements of your personality may need to be amplified or tempered depending on the situation.

- **CliftonStrengths:** All 177 questions in this assessment are carefully calibrated to reveal what you naturally do best. The results you'll receive at the end of the process show you how to develop your greatest talents into strengths and use your personalized results and reports to maximize your potential. The tool also helps you understand the shadow side of your strengths (every strength can be taken to an extreme), so you don't over-index into a negative place. It can be used for general self-knowledge, but it's especially helpful in workplace settings. When entire teams take CliftonStrengths, they can request reports that cross-reference their talents and tendencies, showing how they can most effectively collaborate to make the most of their individual and shared strengths.

- **Enneagram:** Introduced at the beginning of this chapter, the Enneagram test was first created by Bolivian philosopher Oscar Ichazo in the late 1960s. It's designed to help us see ourselves at a deeper, more objective level and can be valuable to our quest for self-knowledge. It offers both a basic personality type as well as motivators, coping mechanisms, behaviors, attitudes, and defenses.

- **HEARTI:** Developed by PrismWork, HEARTI stands for the six foundational skills leaders need to build best-in-class cultures: humility, empathy, accountability, resiliency, transparency, and inclusivity. The development tool uplevels any leader's understanding of their own twenty-first-century readiness and which HEARTI traits are their strengths and areas for growth. The assessment takes fifteen minutes.

- **Self-reflect and self-evaluate:** This practice is a fantastic way to complement the more structured and generalized self-reflection tools. It's also something you can do immediately, without investment, and however feels best to you. Journal or document your experiences, feelings, triggers, wins, and challenges and put them into perspective. Start simple: think back over the previous week and consider when you were anxious versus when you were in flow. Which meetings went well or terribly, and why? What could you have done differently? This can also be where mindfulness comes in. Take the time to reflect and be present rather than constantly moving from one task to the next.

Learn to Listen Deeply

Truly self-aware leaders are confident enough to know they don't know all the answers.

Daniel Lubetzky, CEO of Kind, is often attributed as having said, "We need to understand the other side to impact the other side. We become much more effective as humans and leaders when we engage in hearty conversations with those who are different from us, not necessarily to change our opinions, but to build the empathy muscle."

Self-aware leaders seek out new perspectives, pursue new ways of looking at challenges, and make space for other points of view. To cultivate these skills, leaders must first learn to put their egos aside and listen deeply, a practice that involves both remaining open to outside input *and* tapping into self-awareness. Doing this also enables them to practice empathy as we defined it earlier: seeing, understanding, and (where appropriate) feeling another person's perspective and then using that information to act compassionately.

When I spoke with social change entrepreneur and founder of the 3% Movement Kat Gordon about the importance of self-awareness in leadership, she was eager to tell me about psychologist Tara Brach's philosophy of deep listening. "Brach points out that when you're having a disagreement or a moment of tension with someone, the act of listening to them is critically important, but so is self-listening," Gordon told me. "If you respond immediately with what comes up in your own mind, you're likely to regret it. Deep listening means giving yourself the time and space to react thoughtfully instead of letting your first thoughts blindly steer the car."

Gordon further explained that deep listening involves paying attention to your own inner dialogue so you can create room for reparation even before you address the other person's concerns. It's a practice that helps leaders stay flexible and avoid relying on fixed, panicky responses when in crisis.

Letting go of your
ego and being curious
enough to learn and
grow is a sure sign that
you are truly tapping
into your empathy.

Amer Kaissi, author of the brilliant book *Humbitious*, cites surface-level listening as an issue that's tied to an inflated sense of self-importance. In an interview for my podcast, he told me, "If you're a leader and your confidence is much higher than your competence, that's going to be a problem. You're going to come across as arrogant and you won't truly listen to other people. When we think we know everything about everything, we don't allow others to bring in their expertise."

To avoid this behavior, challenge yourself to listen to *understand* instead of just listening to *reply*. Focus fully on the information you're being given so you can absorb and react to it.

Here are some tactics to try:

- **Practice emotional regulation:** Dr. Chris L. Johnson, leadership consultant and author of *The Leadership Pause*, has devoted her life to the deep listening that underpins what matters most in people's lives. When I spoke with her for *The Empathy Edge* podcast, she told me how her techniques for creating mindful pauses and regulating emotions have helped her clients be more clear-headed, feel calmer, connect with the people around them, even see a bigger vision. Through breathing exercises, recentering, and cultivating awareness of our physical selves and reactions, Dr. Johnson shows leaders across industries how to prepare themselves for deep listening. She taught me that beginning to pause is a full-body practice. It is about dropping out of our monkey mind and dropping into the body and the sensations that allow us to shift gears.

- **Listen to understand:** As a leader, it's easy to slip into the habit of listening as a courtesy as you wait to reply. You allow others to weigh in but assume you know best. When you listen at a surface level and are really just waiting for your turn to speak, you're closing off a path to valuable learning. You're not allowing ideas, input, and constructive criticism to sink in. I can say with utter humility that this inclination of mine has shut me off from truly hearing what others have to say, which is why it's a skill I'm constantly working on! (Top tip: I take notes while another person is talking so I can really ensure I hear them, and I also note questions or points I might make when they are done speaking so I don't forget and can still stay focused on what they are saying.)

- **Focus on service as a leader:** Leaders who listen deeply seldom view themselves as superior to their team members. Instead, their deep listening habits stem from a belief that their own purpose is to serve their team for the larger mission. Or even serve their team members—empowering and supporting them—so those team members can succeed. They view themselves as *servant leaders*. Leadership coaches and former U.S. Marine Corps officers John Buford and Sean Georges coauthored *On Mission*, which frames service leadership by saying, "You're not just walking around patting people on top of the head. You're asking a simple question: What is my best and highest role to serve this person or this team in alignment with our shared mission?" Doing this requires consistent, deep listening.

What You Risk If You Lack Self-Awareness

Across the ten studies that Dr. Tasha Eurich examined to learn more about self-awareness in leadership, she saw two categories emerge. She wrote:

The first, which we dubbed **internal self-awareness**, represents how clearly we see our own values, passions, aspirations, fit with our environment, reactions (including thoughts, feelings, behaviors, strengths, and weaknesses), and impact on others.

The second category, **external self-awareness**, means understanding how other people view us, in terms of those same factors listed above.

Dr. Eurich's research found that internal self-awareness led to higher job and relationship satisfaction, personal and social control—and that it related to lower levels of anxiety, stress, and depression. The team also found that those with high levels of external self-awareness were more skilled at showing empathy, seeing other perspectives, and that they have better, more satisfying relationships with their employees.

Clearly, both types of self-awareness have huge benefits. Dr. Eurich's findings show that leaders who cultivate this pillar are happier, less stressed, and more effective at building trust with their employees.

Lack of self-awareness can be dangerous, causing leaders to exist in an optimism bubble, which is not rooted in the reality of what is going on with their people. When I interviewed Rae Shanahan, chief strategy officer at Businessolver, which puts out the annual report on the state of workplace empathy mentioned earlier, she shared her shock at the 2023 report findings. Empathy went off a cliff in terms of the gap between what HR professionals knew to be going on in the organization and the false optimism of CEOs. In particular, the data from HR professionals saw double-digit declines in empathy with a twenty-four-point gap between how HR and CEOs view empathy in each other.

Many CEOs believe their organizations are doing a great job at being empathetic to employee needs, while HR leaders tell a different story. For example, when you force employees back to the office with a month's notice, and they haven't had childcare in place for a few years during the pandemic, that creates a situation that is not feasible. "If a CEO is not self-aware, it can lead to denial because they're not actually listening and giving credence to what people are going through," Shanahan said. "Many of the CEOs were overly optimistic about everything. They're thinking that everybody wants to go back to [the office]. And this is not representative of the struggles and the challenges facing their people. But HR professionals are the ones that are saying this whole thing about 'my CEO being empathetic is hypocritical.'"

I'd add that self-aware leaders are better able to set healthy boundaries and avoid burnout than leaders who plow through life with little self-reflection. Understanding your own emotions, leadership style, and triggers helps you see when you need to pull back, be firmer, manage your time more carefully, take time off, and create other constraints that protect your well-being.

Jamie Greenwood, who weighed in earlier, points out that while boundaries are crucial, many people-focused leaders are fearful of setting them. "What I've seen in the last fifteen years—particularly among women leaders—is that they're very concerned about causing harm," she said. "And they are equally concerned with harm being done to them. They are concerned about retaliation. They worry that if they set a boundary, even if it's well intentioned, it may be taken the wrong way and they will get in trouble. It often feels safer to say nothing, have no boundaries, and just be an endless giver."

That's an express ticket to leadership misery and burnout. If you start cultivating self-awareness, you'll have the confidence and poise to set the boundaries you need to continue leading empathetically and effectively.

Workplace boundaries are a crucial and often-overlooked component of our next pillar, Self-Care. In the coming chapter, we'll dive into the myriad reasons why leaders with ongoing, strategic self-care practices are experts at avoiding burnout so they maintain the capacity to practice empathy more effectively.

Everyday Empathy Check-In: Self-Awareness

Let's get real and honest with ourselves to cultivate self-awareness. Here are some questions to guide you:

- Every *morning* ask yourself: What is my intention for today?

- Every *morning* ask yourself: At the end of the day, what do I want to have accomplished? What do I need to do today to make the day worthwhile?

- Every *evening* ask yourself: What was my general mood today? (Angry? Anxious? Calm?) What set me off? How did that mood impact my interactions? Are there any relationships I need to repair tomorrow?

- Every *evening* ask yourself: Was there a moment when I felt I was doing my best today? Was there a moment I'm not proud of? Why?

Top tip: These are also great journal prompts!

For more prompts and free resources to help you shore up your own self-awareness, please head to TheEmpathy Dilemma.com/Resources.

Chapter Highlights

- Self-awareness supports empathetic leadership by enabling leaders to understand how their character and behaviors influence their own actions as well as team dynamics.

- Self-awareness builds trust through accountability, and it helps leaders remain open to change and promote learning and development among team members.

- Many leaders overlook self-awareness by prioritizing external tasks and crises. However, studies show that self-reflection enhances leadership effectiveness. It also can result in lowered stress, anxiety, and depression, and it leads to better decision-making, stronger relationships, and improved organizational performance.

- Strengthen both internal and external self-awareness. Effective leaders take time to practice introspection and also actively seek input from others to uncover blind spots and gain a more accurate understanding of themselves and their behaviors.

SELF-CARE

Set Boundaries. Fill Your Tank. Recharge Your Most Precious Asset.

"As leaders, we're other-focused and all in service. And what I've learned, at least in my own journey, is that if you're not willing to express that same level of kindness and empathy toward yourself and what you're going through, it's not going to be sustainable."
MARLY Q CASANOVA, inspirational speaker, leadership trainer, community-builder

What Is Self-Care? Enforcing strong boundaries, taking time to recharge, delegating, resting, and stewarding one's own mental health as a leader.

Why Is Self-Care Important? Depleted leaders are ineffective leaders. It can be tempting to shoulder additional burdens in the name of empathy, but in the end you are doing yourself and your team a disservice. True empathy means treating yourself as empathetically as you should your employees. It means getting your own house in order so you have the capacity to meet other perspectives with curiosity, not defensiveness or fear.

FORMER NEW ZEALAND prime minister Jacinda Ardern has a lot of impressive accomplishments under her belt. She became the youngest female head of government in the world when she was elected in 2017 at the age of thirty-seven. Just one year later she became the second elected world leader to give birth while in office. (Pakistan's Benazir Bhutto was the first.) Ardern steered her country through the COVID-19 pandemic, the recession that followed, the White Island volcanic eruption, and the tragic mosque shootings in Christchurch. I admit to being completely in awe of this amazing leader and how empathetically she handled crises. To me, she is the model of a strong empathetic leader.

But many people may remember her exit from office more than they remember all she achieved while holding the highest seat in all of New Zealand. In January 2023, after nearly six years as PM, she announced that she was simply too burned out to continue.

"I believe that leading a country is the most privileged job anyone could ever have but also one of the more challenging," Ardern said during her resignation speech. "You cannot and should not do it unless you have a full tank plus a bit in reserve for those unexpected challenges."

She's hardly the first public figure to cite exhaustion and burnout as the reason for stepping back. Over the past few years we've seen Fall Out Boy guitarist Joe Trohman announce he was "stepping away" from the wildly popular band to steward his mental health. Tennis prodigy Naomi Osaka was at the top of her game when she announced she needed a break from the sport in 2021. Gymnast Simone Biles withdrew from the team competition and the individual all-around competition at the Tokyo Olympics in 2021 due to stress and overwhelm. And in 2022 alone, Amazon, Starbucks, Pinterest, and American Airlines saw their CEOs resign.

Clearly, career-ending burnout can strike even the highest of performers and achievers.

Burnout is increasingly on the radar of wellness experts and physicians too. In 2019, the World Health Organization acknowledged burnout as an official medical diagnosis, and scores of studies show that employment-related burnout can negatively impact your mental and physical health. *Harvard Business Review* offers a staggering list of possible effects, including "coronary artery disease, hypertension, sleep disturbances, depression, and anxiety, as well as increased alcohol and drug use. Moreover, burnout has been shown to produce feelings of futility and alienation, undermine the quality of relationships, and diminish long-term career prospects." All because many leaders, especially those who lean into empathy for their people, feel safer working themselves into poor health than they do showing themselves some compassion.

Despite this evidence, plenty of critics were quick to call Ardern weak and cowardly when she stepped down as prime minister. I'm more inclined to agree with transformation coach Jo Glynn-Smith's assessment. In an interview with *Harper's Bazaar*, she said, "What Jacinda has done takes enormous strength and courage; the ability to set boundaries and know when enough is enough is incredibly refreshing. I hope it encourages others to do the same."

Right on.

In fact, I'd take it a step further and encourage leaders to do everything they can to avoid burnout *before* they hit that "enough is enough" breaking point. For leadership to be sustainable, leaders need to embrace and engage in ongoing self-care to keep themselves safe and sane. They need to show themselves the same empathy they strive so hard to offer their teams.

Much like self-awareness, self-care often gets written off as a luxury. Or as touchy-feely nonsense that "real" leaders shouldn't bother to indulge in. But more and more, experts are encouraging people in leadership roles to take self-care seriously as a matter of sustainability and efficiency. If you run yourself ragged staying up late to answer emails, never break for exercise, and eat nothing but greasy takeout food on the go between meetings, how can you expect yourself to perform well? And perhaps more importantly, how can you expect yourself to keep burnout at bay?

Short answer: you can't.

This is because burnout is the result of deprioritizing self-care. It happens when you drive yourself to exhaustion while coping with an unmanageable workload or lack of boundaries, and it is exacerbated by feeling you lack control of your work or need more support from your colleagues. It's a lack of empathy for yourself, plain and simple. Reclaiming self-care enables you to manage these factors somewhat by conserving your energy and protecting your mental health. For example, time off and effective delegation can mitigate workload and boundary issues; expressing your needs honestly helps you regain a sense of control; and adequate rest boosts your energy, enabling you to more effectively be there for your team.

No one can be expected to think clearly, openly, and empathetically if their own well has run dry.

Now, I know "self-care" has become an Instagram-trendy buzzword, but it is really a requirement for *any* human being. Self-care is about taking care of yourself as your most precious asset. And taking care of yourself looks different for everyone; it's not just the traditionally feminine activities with which it is often associated. Self-care can take a variety of other forms.

Executive coach Monique Valcour recommends "prioritizing good sleep habits, nutrition, exercise, social connection, and practices that promote equanimity and well-being, like meditating, journaling, and enjoying nature." We'll explore other strategies and tactics later in the chapter too. For now, let's just agree that for empathetic leaders, self-care cannot be considered a luxury. It's one of the only tools we've got to stop burnout before it takes hold.

How Does Self-Care Benefit Empathetic Leaders?

Burnout is a *huge* risk for empathetic leaders, especially now. In a post-COVID world, people-centric leaders who focus on compassion are expected to take on even more duties, support their teams in new ways, and be increasingly agile. One issue I hear again and again is that leaders feel compelled to act as counselors and confidants for their team members, and it's draining away their much-needed focus.

"We're squeezing these managers, and even colleagues, into roles as mental health specialists," said social change entrepreneur Kat Gordon. "Many of these people are not equipped to provide the right support for the issues their employees are facing. They can actually cause more harm than good."

Businessolver's 2023 *State of Workplace Empathy* report echoes this concern and highlights the voices of business leaders who are feeling the pinch. One HR leader told the report's authors, "I am burning it at both ends of the stick day in and day out since COVID. I'm exhausted. We need to take care of everyone else, but no one is taking care of us."

Far too many leaders are trapped in this draining and totally untenable situation. And it doesn't lead to empathy: it leads to destruction.

Brené Brown sums it up well in her book *Atlas of the Heart*: "Boundaries are a prerequisite for compassion and empathy. We can't connect with someone unless we're clear about where we end and they begin. If there's no autonomy between people, then there's no compassion or empathy, just enmeshment."

I believe the way out isn't necessarily to demand more care from others; it's to learn and practice self-care so you can set those clear boundaries and have reserves in your tank—on an ongoing basis.

In a work context, embracing self-care often involves rethinking how your time gets spent, which means it can be especially beneficial to leaders who get sucked into the crises of others or feel forced to take on inappropriate workloads. Here are some other ways self-care can support empathetic leaders.

Self-Care Enables Leaders to Set Stricter Boundaries

Teacher, writer, and embodiment coach Prentis Hemphill says, "Boundaries are the distance at which I can love you and me simultaneously." In the workplace, "love" translates to respect, and the boundaries that leaders set enable them to respect and empathize with both themselves and their team members. In other words, creating and enforcing boundaries isn't selfish or strict; it's incredibly healthy! Vital, even. And it provides empathetic leaders with the space, energy, perspective, and flexibility to be productive and compassionate every day.

Self-Care Can Keep Burnout at Bay

Although burnout can be triggered by everything from shifting roles to lack of recognition, multiple studies have cited long hours, relentless stress, and interpersonal drama as some of the most widespread causes. The ability to engage in self-care can protect leaders from driving themselves to the brink. Knowing when to take time away from work combats the effects of working long hours; getting regular exercise reduces stress; and connecting with friends and loved ones can temper the corrosive effects of interpersonal drama. All of which amount to self-focused acts of empathy.

Leaders Who Feel Healthy and Recharged Are More Effective

A 2023 study found that chronic stress can impact cognition and make it harder for leaders to make tough decisions. Proactively managing stress with self-care practices like exercise, meditation, or boundary-setting helps restore clear thinking. On a related note, Sigal Barsade, professor at the Wharton School of the University of Pennsylvania, points out that moods and attitudes are contagious, so how leaders feel and behave has a massive impact on their teams. Committing to self-care practices that create stable moods can

Career-ending burnout can strike even the highest of performers and achievers.

help both leaders and team members stay focused on work and in tune with each other. When leaders feel grounded and settled, they have more capacity to see other people's points of view without feeling anxious or threatened. They can remain curious and open—and yes, see, understand, and (where appropriate) feel another person's perspective, and use that information to act compassionately!

Self-Care Puts Priorities in Focus

Based on my research and interviews, I believe leaders who value their own well-being are more likely to act according to their core values. They know that a relentless, tunnel-vision focus on work isn't only unhealthy, it's unwise. It sets them up to ignore their friends, family, hobbies, personal goals, and all the interests that support their sense of self. Empathetic leaders know that self-care practices are valuable because they serve as reminders to gut-check their priorities. They force analytical questions such as "Is this more important than my health?" "Can this wait so I can recharge and tackle it with my full attention?" "Am I showing myself the same empathy I show my team?" and "How can I balance my time more effectively?"

Leaders Who Model Self-Care Set Good Examples

People in leadership positions are de facto role models, which means the examples they set and choices they make influence the people they supervise. Those who model self-care set examples for their teams so *they* don't work themselves into oblivion, making everyone less successful. Want to keep your team operating at peak performance? Show them it's safe to take care of their energy and creativity; it's compassionate and an important way to prevent burnout at all levels.

As Guy Weismantel, technology CEO and growth leader, pointed out, "If I am not making time for myself, my tension and stress come out to my team. So if I am not taking that time, I'm actually not doing myself or them a service."

It can feel hard to carve out space in your life and career for self-care, but doing so puts you on the path to leading more empathetically. Read on to find out how you can continually build on this pillar every single day.

How to Incorporate More Self-Care

Don't go thinking that self-care only happens on vacation days. The self-care you undertake as a leader can show up both at the office and at home. Jessica Gold, chief wellness officer at the University of Tennessee System, suggests establishing both short-term and long-term self-care practices. This will help you steward your own well-being sustainably until it becomes second nature.

That is easier said than done, but it's important to minimize our stress and positively impact our overall well-being. Gold wrote, "Focus on day-to-day things you can control: your reaction to things, how you're feeling and how you treat yourself and your loved ones." She recommends that you "acknowledge how you are feeling, reflect upon your emotions and then move forward."

"Eventually avoiding your feelings catches up to you, so it's better to acknowledge the hard emotions, the good emotions and that both exist at the same time," Gold wrote. "You move forward by recognizing and understanding the emotions you are experiencing and your reactions."

What can you do to make sure self-care is *always* part of your practice?

Honor Who You Are

When leaders stay in touch with who they are and what they represent, that goes a long way toward taking care of themselves. Those who try to be someone they're not end up negatively impacting their mental health; those who show up as themselves and understand how they operate are better able to enforce their preferences and limitations. This ties back to the Self-Awareness Pillar, but it also manifests as self-care.

I spoke with Claude Silver for my podcast, and she shared an amazing story about leaders honoring themselves at her company. Silver is chief heart officer at VaynerMedia, working alongside marketer and bestselling author Gary Vaynerchuk. Vaynerchuk is a highly charismatic figure who looms large at the company, and in her first few years there, Silver noticed that employees were bending over backwards to emulate him. They'd tell her, "I want to be just like Gary, but I can't work eighteen hours a day. I'm trying to hustle harder, but I can't work like that."

She put their minds at ease. "I said, 'Gary does that because he loves it. His work is a hobby; this is what he does. But you want to go play soccer on the weekends, and it's really important for you to carve that time out.' I tried to help empower people to have conversations with their managers around set work hours and boundaries," Silver said. "I told them, 'You've got to go be you. It's great to look up to people and learn from them. But there's a reason we chose you. Let's figure out how to amplify all of your leadership skills.'"

Minter Dial, author of *You Lead*, told me, "We're no longer in touch with who we are and what we represent and what we stand for. You need to actually have empathy for yourself. You need to understand and accept who you are. Are you showing up? Are you on time? Are you real with yourself? Are you reflecting everything about you? Are you aware of your baggage?"

Being constantly stressed and trying to fit yourself into a box is self-defeating. When you honor who you are, you're going to be more open to listening to new ideas, hearing people out, reading body language, and other acts of empathy.

Here are some tactics to try:

- **Work with a coach:** Honoring who you are starts with knowing who you are, which can be surprisingly challenging! If you can tell that your leadership style runs contrary to your work culture but aren't sure *how*, consider working with an executive coach to unearth some insights. A good coach will also help you formulate strategies to bring your whole self into your work. It works for high-performance and competitive athletes, so why shouldn't it work for you?

- **Know your triggers:** All of us have situations and language that cause us to feel unwieldy emotions and pull us out of our authentic selves. Recognizing these provocations makes it easier to manage them. Do you struggle when team members ask too many procedural questions while ignoring strategy? Do you feel like you'll blow your top every time colleagues name-drop industry players? To honor who you are, you need to understand the things that make you behave out of character so you can create behavioral strategies ahead of time.

Seek Support and Advice

Along with boundaries, exercise, and other individual self-care practices, leaders can benefit tremendously from seeking peer support. Feeling understood by those in similar situations goes a long way toward alleviating work stress and cultivating self-compassion. Peer support groups, trusted advisors/mentors, and people who can serve as objective sounding boards are priceless to leaders grappling with

Self-care isn't just about resting. It's also about recharging, gaining a new perspective, engaging your mind or heart in a different way, and finding joy in your life.

complex challenges and issues. It's a way to learn best practices from people who truly understand where you are. (I offered a similar suggestion in the chapter on self-awareness, but in the context of self-care, it's more about finding support than assessing strengths and weaknesses.)

Robert Russman Halperin, a researcher at MIT's Center for Collective Intelligence, wrote, "[Peer support groups] allow participants to share concerns, show vulnerability, hear different viewpoints, clarify priorities, and make decisions with greater confidence. Members also build camaraderie and form connections that help them feel safe, grounded, and capable in a volatile and uncertain world. The support they receive in forums sustains them through their toughest professional (and personal) challenges and fosters their long-term success."

It's such a relief to have a person or community where you can admit what you don't know and find help. Or even just let off steam! Most of the successful empathetic leaders I've spoken to have this type of relationship in place, either informally or formally.

Here are some tactics to try:

- **Find a mentor:** Caring for yourself as a leader can feel like an uphill battle, but it's made far less challenging when you have someone looking out for your best interests. Developing a relationship with a mentor, ideally someone you can meet with regularly, gives you a sounding board and continuous feedback loop that you can trust. This doesn't even have to be a professional mentor. Just someone you trust and admire who can make sure your self-care practices don't get neglected.

- **Assemble a personal advisory board:** Yep, you *do* recognize this tactic from the previous chapter; it works well for both self-awareness and self-care! As a leader, you can create your own peer support group, mastermind group, or peer-to-peer coaching circle to help you see and overcome challenges. This can be a formal group or an ad hoc, casual one with trusted peers that meets regularly.

- **Consider connecting with a personal therapist:** I know that this recommendation may feel a little uncomfortable for some people. But the fact is that you don't park your humanity at the office door; there's a lot that you bring into your work that is not work-related. And so potentially, to take care of yourself, there might be things you need to talk about or vent about to an unbiased third party. Someone who isn't a work colleague or family member. The good news about the evolution of our workplace culture is that we're having more candid conversations in regard to therapy and its benefits. If you believe that personal issues or past traumas could be getting in the way of your performance as a leader or could be getting in the way of how you show up at work, give some thought to connecting with a personal therapist. Perhaps your company health plan even offers this important benefit.

Recharge and Renew

Taking time off, moving your body, making space for your personal life, and finding ways to truly rest are all practices with proven health benefits. But for years, leaders felt like they were indulgences instead of necessities.

"Historically, leaders had to show their commitment by working all hours or being available at all times," said business builder and C-suite technology executive Dave Zinman. "And the unintended consequence was that they felt they had to respond to every request from every employee. Even if that meant being so overwhelmed and stressed yourself that you had to answer emails and put out fires over the weekend. You couldn't escape the work."

Many leaders have seen their corporate cultures shift to embrace the importance of rest and renewal. If you happen to be in a company that still resists flexible vacation scheduling or ample paid time off, there are other ways to recharge after tough days. What gives you energy? What nourishes your soul? Reading, skiing, kickboxing, meditating, crossword puzzles, writing, drawing, working with your hands, gardening, spending time with your kids? Whether you crave something restful or something more active to recharge your batteries, make time in your schedule to pursue the activities that light you up, bring you joy, and replenish your energy.

Here are some tactics to try:

- **Use your paid time off (PTO):** Obvious? Yes. But worth hammering home? Also yes! Far too many leaders feel like they can't use their vacation days or will fall too far behind if they take time off. And that leads to resentment, decreased productivity, and burnout. If you can't fathom taking a two-week vacation, try spreading out some days off. Give yourself every other Monday away from work, or the last Friday of each month. And make sure you detach completely from work when you do. You plug your phone in to recharge and you as a human are no different! Plus, your team will take their cue on self-care from your behavior, so make sure you are being a good role model and that your actions (not just your words) show this is what the team values.

- **Set hard boundaries around time at home:** This one is tough but ever so important. Unless you work in a field where actual lives are on the line, consider telling your company that you won't take calls or respond to emails after, say, 7 p.m. on weeknights or at all on the weekends.

True emergencies may slip through occasionally, of course, but just setting this parameter can help you protect valuable recharging time. Make emergencies the rare exception and the choice of last resort for your team, not the norm.

- **Embrace your non-work interests:** Here's the thing about hobbies—they sound like practices that only non-parents working part-time jobs could ever undertake, but they're actually super important for most adults. Multiple studies have shown that engaging in a pastime you truly enjoy can result in reduced stress, enhanced well-being, improved social connection, and decreased depression and anxiety. Remember, self-care isn't just about resting. It's also about recharging, gaining a new perspective, engaging your mind or heart in a different way, and finding joy in your life. Activities like cycling, knitting, rock-climbing, volunteering with animals, making art or music, journaling, and martial arts can do all those things and more.

On that last note, women's leadership coach Jamie Greenwood taught me something I want to pass along to you: there's a huge difference between self-care and self-maintenance.

"Manicures and massages aren't self-care; they're self-maintenance," she explained. "Self-care is a way of being and a way of growing and a way of living into our lives, which getting our nails done doesn't even begin to cover."

Along with other coaches and mental health experts, Greenwood believes that self-care practices support your health and growth over the long term—practices like eating healthy, going to therapy, meditating, setting boundaries, engaging in creativity or play, creating a regular sleep schedule, and exercising. Buying yourself a fancy latte might help you feel less stressed for an hour, but rest and mindfulness practices will help you feel less stressed over your entire career.

And less stress in your life means more energy, openness, and capacity to show empathy toward those you lead.

What You Risk If You Don't Take Care of Yourself

"When we experience stress for an extended time without being able to alter, change, or ameliorate it, we can begin to feel empty, numb, devoid of motivation, hopeless, and beyond caring," said Robert Ciampi, LCSW therapist, quoted in a *Forbes* interview. "A person can get so burned out they become apathetic about everything, including self-care, which could lead to serious illness."

Remember, our goal is empathy. Absolutely *not* apathy!

The Mayo Clinic backs Ciampi up, listing insomnia, substance misuse, heart disease, high blood pressure, and type 2 diabetes as possible side effects of chronic stress and burnout. Learning to embrace self-care could quite literally save your life.

But even if you don't end up seriously ill, you can still feel plenty of other negative repercussions if you neglect self-care. And you will definitely not have anything left in your tank to give to others in terms of active listening, holding space, or being able to see their point of view. When I spoke to Amanda Carlson-Phillips, chief performance innovation officer at corporate well-being, professional development, and sport performance company Exos, she reminded me that holistic stewardship of both mind and body is critical. It helps us stay focused, perform at a higher level, and conserve our energy for important tasks.

"When we think about what it takes to be at our best, we have to optimize our biology and our psychology," she said. "The brain and the body are inextricably linked. And so when we think about human physiology, both mental and physical, it's an act of self-care."

As we've discussed, setting and enforcing healthy boundaries can be an important part of self-care at work. Without strong boundaries and the strength to carve out time for yourself, you risk becoming a pushover as a leader. Higher-ups may take advantage of your time, and team members may learn to manipulate your willingness to compromise.

"Being empathetic doesn't mean giving people everything they want," said Rebecca Friese, cofounder of workplace innovation consultancy FLYN. "Instead, it means listening to understand and working within that context. Creating solutions, organization-wide or individually, that are fit for purpose and mutually beneficial, instead of just caving in."

And, of course, without clear boundaries you may end up overextending yourself. As many leaders have said throughout this chapter, without the ability to say no to unreasonable demands, you may find yourself drowning in work that could and should be handled by others. And you lose the ability to say yes when your time and energy is needed most, such as on connection, conversation, or recharging your own batteries. Empathy is not what makes someone a pushover. Stress, burnout, and insecurity are the real culprits.

But perhaps most importantly, you risk losing your resilience. If, as a leader, you ignore self-care as a regular, personal practice, you won't just get burned out, you'll get worn down. You'll become so depleted that when something minor goes wrong or some piece of criticism hits the wrong way, you'll struggle to recover. When you've got nothing left to give and no energy left to spare, everything feels like an insurmountable crisis. And that makes you turn inward in self-preservation, rather than outward in empathy. How can I listen attentively and see your point of view when I'm struggling to survive myself?

When you practice self-care, you build resilience. You intentionally calm your system to be more adaptable, so you can train yourself to not take things so personally; you can quickly get back up after falling down. That resilience enables you to be tough in the face of harsh words, differing opinions, or bad news. Not so thick-skinned that you become callous (we don't want to lose our empathy completely), but so you remain confident in yourself to face setbacks with a flexible growth mindset rather than fall apart.

At its core, self-care is a kind of self-protection. It shields you from draining yourself dry and growing to resent your work. In the coming chapter, we'll pivot to another pillar that empathetic leaders can use to stay engaged and effective: Clarity.

Everyday Empathy Check-In: Self-Care

- What is your plan for a mental break? Put it in your calendar!

- Am I getting enough sleep?

- Did I eat meals and snacks today, or did I let myself get famished?

- What can I build into my day to nourish my mind, body, or soul? Is there an activity I can plan or a moment of joy?

- What does it feel like in my body when I am triggered or provoked? What strategies can I deploy when I recognize those negative feelings arising?

- What does my body, mind, and spirit need today?

For more prompts and free resources to help you shore up your own self-care, please head to TheEmpathyDilemma .com/Resources.

Chapter Highlights

- Burnout is a significant risk for empathetic leaders, and self-care plays a crucial role in preventing it. Leaders like former New Zealand prime minister Jacinda Ardern have shown the importance of knowing when to prioritize their well-being.

- Self-care enables empathetic leaders to set stricter boundaries, which allows them to respect and empathize with themselves and their team members. It provides leaders with the space, energy, perspective, and flexibility to be productive and compassionate.

- Engaging in self-care helps mitigate factors such as long hours, relentless stress, and interpersonal conflicts. Taking time off, exercising, and maintaining social connections all contribute to recharging body, mind, and spirit to protect leaders from driving themselves to exhaustion.

- Leaders who prioritize self-care are more effective in their roles. Proactively managing stress and maintaining stable moods through self-care practices enhance leaders' decision-making abilities and positively influence their teams.

- Incorporating self-care into leadership styles requires honoring one's authentic self, seeking support and advice from peers, and regularly recharging and renewing.

- By prioritizing self-care, leaders can maintain their health, stay focused on their core values, and prevent negative repercussions such as becoming a pushover or losing resilience.

CLARITY

Don't Assume We All Understand the Assignment

"Clarity paves the way for empathy. Because if you're totally unclear—and believe me, people are far less clear than they think they are—you're not on the same page, you're not on the same wavelength. How can you even begin to be empathetic? You end up making requests, wasting team members' time and energy, and never recognizing that that's what you've done."
ANN LATHAM, author of *The Power of Clarity*, *The Disconnect Principle*, and *The Clarity Papers*

What Is Clarity? Ensuring everyone is on the exact same page through clear communication, expectations, feedback, and understanding of job roles, all of which roll up to an actionable mission statement and meaningful company values.

Why Is Clarity Important? Resentments build where misunderstandings thrive. One of the biggest reasons leaders and workers butt heads is lack of communication on mission, roles, and responsibilities. When people know what's expected of them—including in emergencies and on an as-needed basis—they are less likely to become disgruntled or even feel entitled. Clarity helps people feel seen, heard, and valued; reduces the likelihood of conflict; and enables everyone to work together more effectively.

CLARITY IS *so* underrated. And woefully underused.

Sure, plenty of leaders talk a good game about its importance, but plenty more shy away from actually creating clarity when things get diplomatically dicey. Or they believe that clarity is a one-way street flowing from themselves toward their team members. They're scratching the surface without tapping into the true power of this pillar.

And they're certainly failing to leverage clarity as a form of compassion. For clarity to connect back to empathy, it must be both genuine and reciprocal.

Jonni Ressler, CEO of marketing consultancy Eleven 11 Solutions, knows this all too well. As a leader who is dedicated to practicing empathy, she's seen how clarity can make or break an interaction. With clients, partners, and employees alike, she's learned to set communication ground rules when she senses that a conversation might be fraught or tense.

"Just yesterday I read an email that was super inflammatory and said a bunch of things that weren't true," she told me. "It essentially accused me of not delivering on time. So I reached out to the client and asked for five minutes on the phone. I told them, 'I'd like to explain what I'm experiencing, then the floor is yours. I want to acknowledge that some of the things I'm going to say might make you feel defensive. But if you can give me five minutes to say what I need to, after that we'll have a full conversation.'"

Amazing, right? In just a few sentences, Ressler asked for what she needed, recognized that her comments might be hard to hear, and set a boundary around saying her piece. Radical clarity: established.

From there, she read the email aloud over the phone and explained her concerns. She said much of what the client had written wasn't factually true and then walked through the various deadlines and dates that both parties had documented. Instead of indignation or false bravado, she vulnerably admitted the accusations being leveled at her made her feel defensive and scared, so she wanted to get on the phone to discuss that.

"I told them, 'So much of what's been said in this email isn't accurate, but I know you sent it because something is happening or changing on your side. Still, I want you to know where I'm sitting.'"

After that, and with the facts of the situation outlined, the client realized they'd gotten the delivery dates wrong. (Really wrong. Like seven months wrong.) Seeing they'd jumped the gun, they apologized to Ressler, and they were able to refocus on successfully getting the work done together.

This is clarity that leaves room for empathy. Ressler laid the groundwork for expressing what she was experiencing and what she needed, and she also created space for the client to talk about their own experiences and needs. Everyone had a chance to vent and communicate, feeling safe to do so. Knowing herself as she did (self-awareness) and having navigated similarly challenging conversations before, Ressler was up front and firm about explaining her perspective first. But she also knew that the client would need to explain their own context and that she should promise to be a good listener in return.

It takes a lot of practice to model empathetic clarity, but it's worth the effort—both because it improves work relationships and because it bolsters work results. Clarity ensures we are all on the same page as to expectations and next steps. It removes guesswork and stress.

In short, clarity is a form of kindness.

In fact, I have often stated that most conflicts stem from unclear—or unspoken—communication. If we could all just sit down, spell things out, and honestly talk things through, we wouldn't run into so many false assumptions that spin up into unnecessary drama. And worse, failed initiatives that leave a trail of resentment in their wake.

Recent research proves this theory of mine correct.

Research conducted by the Economist Intelligence Unit reveals that 86 percent of senior executives, managers, and junior staff at U.S. companies encounter communication breakdowns that lead to losses in productivity, missed project deadlines, and sales deals that don't close.

That's a big price to pay, right? Maybe if we spent more time bolstering clear and compassionate communication, we'd need fewer draconian cost-saving measures like laying people off, cutting benefits, or skimping on customer service.

If those leaders were able to express their ideas and expectations with real clarity, they could stem the tide of those costly losses. In fact, further research by the Harris Poll on behalf of Grammarly shows that 72 percent of business leaders believe effective communication has increased their team's productivity, and 52 percent of knowledge workers agree.

That same report emphasizes that clarity in written communication is increasingly important in a remote-work world. Harris found that 80 percent of workers and 93 percent of business leaders say their ability to get work done is tied to how well their collaborators communicate their needs and share their ideas. As we spend less time together in person, the ability to convey expectations, information, and boundaries in writing will become ever more important.

Especially to those of us who truly value empathy. I made clarity a Pillar of Effective Empathetic Leadership because if you're not clear, you're not being empathetic.

Far too many people believe that sugarcoating difficult information is the empathetic way. But doing so brings the risk of omitting information, confusing the recipient, or making false assumptions about their needs and preferences. Sugarcoating is more about *you* than it is about the person you're communicating with; it's your way of (ineffectively) protecting yourself from the potential social blowback of a challenging interaction.

That's not empathy, that's fear.

There's a way to deliver tough information with compassion and candor. It requires us as leaders to both stand our ground and be respectful of any reaction we might receive. And sometimes to ask prompting questions to help the person on the receiving end respond in a healthy and productive way. It often means saying things like, "I'm sure this is a lot for you to process, and I completely understand. What do you need right now? Do you need to go home and think about it? Do you want to rant and blow off some steam? How can I help?"

As empathetic leaders, it's also our responsibility to ensure that what we're saying is fully understood. If the recipient is not taking it in, no matter how clear we think we're being, it's still our responsibility as the communicator to clarify. That's the empathetic imperative.

And it's an imperative that works at work, as well as at home. Recently I was driving in the car with my nine-year-old son, and he was venting about a miscommunication he had at school with another student. He said, "It's his fault he didn't understand what I was saying." Immediately, I said, "Actually, if he didn't understand something you said, the responsibility is on you, the communicator. You may not have been clear enough about what you felt or needed. That's why you need to check in and make sure the other person really understood what you meant."

He didn't love this answer. But it's the truth and something he's working on, along with all of us adults.

Fortunately, clear communication is a practice that doesn't just help us lead our teams more compassionately. It also helps us perform better, enforce our boundaries, and avoid burnout. Let's explore how.

How Does Clarity Benefit Empathetic Leaders?

My very first job out of college was at a large global management consultancy. As soon as I was hired, they shared a career path with clear and codified steps I'd need to follow to get promoted. I started as an analyst, and once I hit certain performance thresholds, I could become a consultant. Same for the pathway to manager and associate partner; eventually, a culmination of years worked and accomplishments achieved would make me a partner. The company even outlined approximately how many years it would take me to move through this progression of promotions. From the moment I got hired, I knew that if I stayed with the company, didn't screw up, and delivered on my work, I could become a partner in possibly ten to fifteen years.

Being offered this level of detail and clarity was incredibly unusual. All the other jobs I'd interviewed for as a recent grad had offered me vague job descriptions and wishy-washy promises of advancement. Nothing even close to this was given to me anywhere else, and it made me feel like the management consultancy understood what a young person just entering the workforce wanted and needed to succeed. They knew that I wouldn't have much experience with office dynamics and would benefit from knowing the ground rules. (Things like, "Don't even start asking about a pay raise/ promotion until you've completed X projects.") They saw that all new employees would benefit from knowing what they needed to do to get to the next level.

The clarity they offered me from day one showed me that they wanted me to succeed. That they wanted *everyone* at the company to succeed. And they'd invested the empathy and compassion necessary to find out how to make that success possible across the board.

By the way, this is what Gen Z expects in the workplace from everyone now. They want to know what's next. This is often mistaken for premature entitlement, but remember our generational expert, consultant, and keynote speaker Anna Liotta stated back in Chapter 3 that this is actually a Gen Z operational code.

Company-wide clarity such as this can *only* come from leaders who recognize the value of open, respectful communication. And as I mentioned earlier, those leaders can reap some incredible rewards in return! Here are some ways that embodying the Clarity Pillar of Effective Empathetic Leadership will benefit leaders.

Clarity Builds Trust and Loyalty

Leaders who offer unclear direction, murky performance feedback, or confusing course-correction make their team members feel lost. Or worse, disrespected. Leaders who practice real clarity—including on boundaries, expectations, and performance issues—experience the opposite. According to the Workforce Institute at UKG, employees value managers who are dependable (52 percent) and honest (34 percent), and capable of delivering helpful feedback (25 percent). When you offer clarity to your employees, they feel trusted and they trust you in return.

Clarity Reduces Conflict

When people understand expectations, they have a far easier time navigating their work responsibilities and collaborating with their colleagues. When you lead with ongoing and genuine clarity, you enable your employees to feel confident in their roles and empowered to manage their challenges. They know who they are in the context of the entire team, so they know how to comport themselves even in the face of conflict. Just imagine how much easier your life would be if your team could cruise through tasks, meetings, and quarterly goals with less friction because everyone is operating from the same playbook.

Being a Clear Communicator
Helps Leaders Maintain Boundaries

The leaders most likely to get saddled with tons of extra responsibility are the ones who can't express their needs. The leaders who practice empathy on themselves by being super clear about their boundaries are better able to delegate, balance their workloads, and avoid burnout.

Remember Jonni Ressler's story from the beginning of this chapter? Being detailed, explicit, and extremely clear with her client benefited the relationship overall, and it helped her protect herself. She didn't open up a free-for-all dialogue about the issue, but instead she made sure that she got to fully express herself *before* the client could interject. Expert boundary-enforcement deployed with empathy. (Which also ticks the self-care box!)

Women's leadership coach Jamie Greenwood also had a great insight about this connection. She told me, "Many people think setting a boundary means that they're a jerk. It's all about how you do it. Being clear actually is very kind. And boundaries, when set properly and appropriately, are just clarity."

Modeling Clarity Encourages Clarity

As with all of the Pillars of Effective Empathetic Leadership, clarity is a behavior that leaders can model and subsequently expect to spread. Being clear with your team members helps them feel safe being clear about their *own* needs, concerns, ideas, and challenges. Communicating with them at a level that shows how much you trust and value them helps them grow as professionals.

So just how do you make sure you're being as clear as possible with your team? Let's find out.

How to Incorporate More Clarity

Ann Latham, president of the consulting firm Uncommon Clarity, said, "The definition of clarity is knowing exactly what you're trying to accomplish with specificity, how you're going to get there, what are the intermediate outcomes that lead to the big outcome, and how to focus so that you can use all of your powers to go one step at a time towards a goal."

All true, but also a tall order, am I right?

It can be tough to gauge your own levels of clarity in communication, which makes it tough to know if they need

Clarity ensures we are all on the same page as to expectations and next steps. It removes guesswork and stress. In short, clarity is a form of kindness.

adjusting. But the hard truth is that very, very few leaders are so skillfully and consistently clear that they can't use some improvement. (And clarity about the unknown is just as important. You may not have all the answers right now, but you can be honest about this and also be clear by offering frequent status updates and laying out the steps needed to get there.)

So with these issues in mind, here are a few checks to perform and strategies to use to ensure you're communicating clearly and empathetically.

Revisit Purpose and Values

Clarity on minutiae won't mean bupkis if your teams don't have foundational clarity on the company's purpose and values. And neither leaders nor employees will be able to act compassionately if the shared purpose and values are confusing or vague. No one will know how responsibilities should be divided or how any work they're doing ladders up to the company's real purpose. Which means confusion, miscommunication, and resentment will infect the entire enterprise. We all need to know exactly what boat we're in and where it's headed! It may take some doing—including reevaluation, discussion, and consensus among leadership—but it's worthwhile. Make your purpose, mission, and values meaningful, not trite, vague statements. And articulate what those look like in *action*: document examples of desired actions, behaviors, or decisions so everyone is clear. Tackle this common clarity issue first.

Vision and mission statements are important, and when phrased well, they can serve as more than just a pretty poster on the wall. They can actually clarify a company's why and give direction as to where we're all going—as well as how we make decisions on a daily basis. Let's look at an example from Patagonia: "We're in business to save our home planet." This vision ensures we all know why we are here and what we're working toward. Your mission statement describes what your teams do on a daily basis to drive your company toward the world described by the vision statement. Another example from Patagonia: "Build the best product, cause no unnecessary harm, and use business to inspire and implement solutions to the environmental crisis." The mission reflects how they are going to make their vision a reality and provides high-level guidance on what the company does and does not do.

Here are some tactics to try:

- **Externalize, organize, focus:** In their book *Farther, Faster, and Far Less Drama*, Janice and Jason Fraser recommend this approach for virtually any issue that requires amassing and filtering input from lots of people. *Externalize* by getting all stakeholders to write possible values on individual sticky notes. *Organize* by grouping the notes according to theme. And *focus* by having everyone vote on the top four to six values that best represent your company.

- **Write or revamp your vision and mission statements:** I do this with my own clients all the time. You want to make your vision and mission statements actionable so they provide a true north for everyone. If they are too fluffy or vague, they don't do you any good. Your vision statement describes an ideal world that would exist if your company's work was entirely successful and no longer needed. (Think of the Patagonia example above.) When you word them clearly, they can be used in daily decisions or strategic meetings to vet important decisions against. If the course of action furthers the mission, it's a go. If it does not, perhaps you need to rethink it.

- **Work with a consultant:** Having worked with giant tech firms and solopreneurs alike, I know exactly how challenging it can be to articulate purpose and values without objective facilitation by an outside expert. If your company can't seem to nail down the verbiage you need to create company-wide clarity, hire a messaging expert. It doesn't have to be me, but bringing in someone with an objective perspective will help you see the forest for the trees.

Clarify Roles and Expectations

How many people review their job descriptions after they've been hired? The number probably approaches zero, except during annual review periods. Given that, consider what you can do to ensure your team members understand and agree to their roles and responsibilities; doing this is incredibly empathetic since it shows you're thinking about the best uses of their time and considering how to balance their duties.

Think beyond the job description to how you can clearly articulate the team's rules of engagement. How does work get done? What is the best way we can communicate with each other? How does each person on the team like to work? Have these discussions. Document them. And ensure you revisit them often to avoid misunderstandings.

One way to approach this is to tune into the language you use on a daily basis. Anna Liotta said, "As leaders, we actually have to be far more explicit about our expectations. We always have to be thinking about our metaphors, our examples, our reference points. We have to make sure that we're creating a mix of those different examples to actually be relevant and resonant in the moment. And we have to be especially careful in using jargon and shorthand; so much clarity gets lost when we fall back on vocabulary that isn't universally known or understood."

Michelle Sherman, an executive leadership coach and the founder of VAST Institute, suggests crafting a code of conduct and using it to build trust and psychological safety so people feel empowered to be their most creative selves. Marketing and design collective Laetro calls this same practice a memorandum of understanding (MOU) on expectations. Creating rules of engagement for your own team allows you to formally codify values and expectations beyond job descriptions, so people have true clarity on their responsibilities. Creative leader Dave Zaboski of Laetro shared his company's extraordinary MOU, and it's so fabulously clear and useful, I wanted to pass it along verbatim (shared with permission, of course).

Laetro Memorandum of Understanding (MOU)

This is a description of the essential nature of the relationships, understandings, and communication between core torchbearers in and around the Laetro ecosystem.

We are a creator collective, and this is our kindred quest: to create, manage, operate, and lovingly grow a creator and technology based company committed to the expansion of human consciousness, creativity, and artistry.

And as such, we walk our talk. We agree to live in integrity and trust, following principles we derive from our collective wisdom. We will live our lives as proof of concept. We agree to be good to each other and practice lightheartedness. We agree to do the work—both outer and inner.

We are creators pulled toward the edges of boundless creativity by our desire to create at the level of what we can imagine. We also know that our road to excellence is our ability to generously collaborate. In this collective endeavor, we agree to get to know each other. We agree to cultivate a confusion tolerance where in the face of ambiguous or inconclusive data, we will refrain from judgment until things become clear. If things aren't clear, we'll clear them up. We will do our best to draw positive energy from each other and promise to be additive. We agree to plus each other. To mentor and be mentored. We are storytellers. We believe. We collaborate. We risk. We iterate and we complete. Everything is going to be okay in the end; if it's not okay, it's not the end.

We agree to pursue and listen for the *yes* as long as it presents itself and we agree to, in good faith, play as hard as possible together for the biggest win. We know things can get difficult; we agree to hold each other to our highest good and agree to never use intimate or vulnerable information for bad.

We believe that now is the time for a greater awakening through collective creativity. We believe in the dynamic balance of heart and mind, science and spirit, the visible and the unseen, the felt and the known. We believe in an expanding universe powered by the only true and real force: love.

I, __[name]__, am with you.

Signature: _____

Date: _____

Here are some tactics to try:

- **Create rules of engagement:** One amazing way to ensure you and your team are on the same page in terms of performance standards and values is to create a set of rules of engagement that everyone can refer to as needed. Forward-thinking leaders call this guiding document by many names. Whether you call it a code of conduct or an MOU, what matters is putting it into practice.

- **Destigmatize ownership discussions:** We've all been in meetings where we've wondered if a certain task or responsibility is ours to own or someone else's. But asking that question point-blank can feel awkward or even accusatory. Piping up to say "Okay, so who owns this?" may sound like you're foisting it off. With decentralized structures on the rise, this problem is only going to worsen if your teams aren't comfortable asking who's doing what.

So give them a mechanism to ask what's theirs and what's not that will quickly alleviate confusion over responsibilities. Make it regular and low pressure so the question never feels loaded and is focused exclusively on clarity of duties. Carve out time during team meetings for people to ask about the breakdown of work or create a Slack channel where queries about task ownership can be discussed. Make these conversations normal and tension-free so everyone feels comfortable asking without bracing for territorialism.

Link Clarity to Accountability

You can't hold people accountable if they're not clear on their expectations and goals. Otherwise, what are they being held accountable to? Everyone on your team should be able to say, "I clearly understand my contribution, I clearly understand that I'm accountable for this piece of the puzzle, and I'm accountable for how I show up every day."

Start by making sure every person you work with understands that accountability means taking ownership of mistakes and working to make things right rather than avoiding conflict or blaming others—and *also* encompasses taking ownership of the purpose and the mission. As leaders, we must be accountable to our teams achieving their goals, and our team members must be clear on how their work ladders up to those goals. Accountability is about more than accepting responsibility when things go wrong. It's about making a proactive commitment to own your role in making things go right.

Claude Silver, chief heart officer at VaynerMedia, told me, "At our company, we are very, very clear. This is what you are expected to do here, and to get that promotion you want, you'll need to do this. That clarity and accountability has removed a big chunk of entitlement, a big chunk of coddling. We encourage people to rise to the challenge through kind candor. Not radical candor, *kind* candor. And that really works for us because ours is a community and culture rooted in kindness."

Here are some tactics to try:

- **Create career progression maps:** Younger members of the workforce especially want to know what's ahead, what's next. It's how they are wired. When you are clear about where current roles can lead and have mapped out a navigable path for them to advance along, you eliminate a lot of angst. You can also tie expectations, accomplishments, and time frames to each phase of the journey to avoid confusion. Check in on progress in weekly one-to-ones or quarterly performance discussions so people always know where they stand.

- **Publicly celebrate and reward milestones:** Now that you've given people a path to follow, be sure you are celebrating progress along the way. This not only encourages your best talent to stay the course, it shows that leadership acknowledges progress and signals to the entire team a strong commitment to development and advancement.

Tell People Why

Leaders are busy and overwhelmed, which means they often convey what needs to be done and when but omit the reason *why*. Author and CEO Nancy Duarte wrote in *Harvard Business Review*, "If your boss comes to you and says, 'I need you to take on this additional project on top of your current workload,' what is your first question going to be? It probably has nothing to do with setting your alarm, rearranging your schedule, or any other version of *how* you're going to get the extra work done. When someone asks you to alter a current behavior, your first question is usually *why*? Because you're not going to try something new or hard unless you're *motivated* to do so."

Lacking a reason why, people feel disrespected or kept in the dark. This amounts to an empathy gap, and one that can be closed quickly and easily with clear explanations for any changes in duties or expectations. They may not like the answer, but at least they understand why the ask is being made.

Here are some tactics to try:

- **Build why into your documentation:** Do you use creative briefs? Project management software? Work orders? Just about any documentation that helps kick off and/or guide a project can include a section that explains why the work is important.

- **Build a culture of why:** Bake in the expectation that team members will offer *why* whenever they embark on a new project or suggest a pivot. Make it clear that people are expected to communicate why whenever they make a decision or change. And encourage everyone to embrace their inner three-year-old by asking *why* multiple times if a reason isn't offered up.

Ask Better Questions

Little-known fact: clarity doesn't come from having the right answer; it comes from asking the right questions. This can include knowing the right prompts when someone approaches you with a concern or problem. How can you assess what your next step is with this person and get *them* to be clear? By asking, "What do you need from me in this moment? Do you need me to offer solutions? Remove an obstacle? Give advice?" A catchy way to say this is "Do you want me to see it, solve it, or support you?"

Ann Latham notes that vague questions (e.g., "How are things going?") can actually make people feel lost, unprepared, and embarrassed since coming up with an intelligent answer on the spot is virtually impossible. Their confidence takes a hit. But she doesn't blame the person on the receiving end at all.

Clarity doesn't come from having the right answer; it comes from asking the right questions.

"People don't realize that it's the question that's at fault," she explained. "When you're asked stupid questions, you'll struggle to respond with great answers. If a leader wants to find out what's going on, they have to ask something specific, something useful. That's the empathetic thing to do."

Here are some tactics to try:

- **Use "I like, I wish, I wonder" to guide conversations:** Potential Squared CEO and author of *Be More Wrong* Colin Hunter shared a great way to deliver clear, compassionate feedback that reduces blame and sets aside ego, while still encouraging problem solving. It also offers an extremely empathetic way to frame clear feedback. He said to use the wording "I like, I wish, I wonder." Here's an example:

  I like that the team is getting really creative on this project and trying new things.

  I wish we could stick closer to the timeline we set out so we can deliver for the launch.

  I wonder what we can do to stay creative but move faster. What might we need to do this?

- **Frame your questions carefully:** Writing about empathy and accountability, executive coach Ed Batista offered this sequence of steps for framing and asking useful questions:

  Connect: Establish and renew the interpersonal connection, followed by an open-ended question.

  Reflect: Having elicited a response, reflect back the essence of the other person's comments.

  Direct: Focus their attention on a particular aspect of their response that invites further exploration.

  Then Ask: Pose a question that builds upon, integrates, or challenges what's been said so far.

- **Ask questions that invite collaboration:** Asking collaborative questions at the beginning of any process or discussion sets a tone of receptivity. When you do this, you're signaling that you are open to new information, approaching the discussion in learning mode, and ready for a multiple-person dialogue. Here are three great ways to frame collaborative questions: "Help me understand..." "Have you considered...?" and "What surprised you?"

Create (and Embrace) a Feedback Loop

Being clear isn't just about how you communicate; it's about how your communication is received. In order to know how people are reacting to your efforts at clarity, you need to both ask them and be prepared to adjust your communication strategies accordingly. Colin Hunter lives this out with his teams and shared this story.

"At an off-site, my team was asked to write things that they appreciate about each person on a flip chart," he said. "And somebody wrote two words on my flip chart: frustrating and confusing. Now, they had the courage to do that. And that's a constructive feedback loop. So since then, I've been noodling, working: how I can remove 'frustrating' and 'confusing' from the vocabulary other people would use about me?"

Here's a tactic to try:

- **Cultivate a culture of honesty:** If you want useful feedback about how clear or unclear you're being, you need to make your team members feel safe sharing their honest opinions. Reinforce verbally that people should feel free to be candid with you, and then back it up by listening and responding to *all* kinds of feedback, including the tough stuff.

Tuning up your leadership clarity can only improve morale, communication, and even performance among team members. When you are clear, people feel safe. They understand the mission, how they can best contribute, and where they stand.

"Clarity and setting expectations have been a big learning lesson and journey for me," said Hilary Hendershott, wealth management advisor and owner of her own firm. "When I started the firm, I thought asking people to do things in a certain way, even though I was paying them, looked bad and wasn't good leadership because I needed to have my team see *me* doing things. But now I see how clarity and process takes almost 100 percent of the drama out of the work and helps people stay accountable when things go wrong."

And, of course, the opposite is also true. Lacking clarity can get leaders into some serious hot water.

What You Risk If You Don't Embrace Clarity

The business risks of unclear communication are well known. Research by Crucial Learning found that 43 percent of workers estimate they waste two weeks (two weeks!) or more thinking about (but not acting on) an unresolved problem at work. Additionally, one-third of employees believe their inability to speak up in tough situations has cost their organizations at least $25,000.

But the costs in trust, social capital, company culture, and interpersonal relationships are potentially even greater. They reach further into the heart of an organization and have both wider repercussions and longer-lasting impact.

For starters, lack of clarity from leaders makes it difficult for team members to stay motivated. If they don't understand what they should be doing or why it matters to the company, they become disconnected from their work. Business builder and C-suite technology executive Dave Zinman has seen this very issue in action.

"When people don't feel seen, heard, or valued, they don't want to do the work," he said. "Sometimes it comes down to the fact that they're not following the same playbook. They need—but lack—a very clear understanding of their roles, what is required of those roles, and what's expected of them."

Leaders who don't express their expectations clearly may see morale and performance diminish, while leaders who don't actively *seek* clarity risk not seeing the full picture. This is the question-asking, truth-seeking side of clarity that Ann Latham referenced in the previous section. An empathetic leader's charge includes both communicating clearly and helping those around them follow suit.

Christopher Mannino learned the value of seeking clarity on the job—a very high-stakes, high-stress job, and one that can make office leadership stressors look pretty tame. He retired as chief of police of the Park Forest Police Department in Park Forest, Illinois, after twenty-five years of service. During his career with the police force, he was a champion of clarity. Now he helps organizations communicate through crises in his role as vice-president of Julie Parker Communications.

Over the years, Mannino saw that his department's approach to juvenile justice was not effective. They were seeing the same kids over and over again, and those kids weren't getting the help or resources they needed to better their situations. So Mannino implemented a program where every child who came into custody at his police department was screened to find out if they were abused or exposed to trauma.

"Under the model of policing I learned, you didn't take the time to find out background details," he said. "But once I realized how effective empathy is for getting to root causes, I wanted to leverage that. We were screening every child to find out why they kept ending up in custody and then help-ing them find resources. Just by asking a few questions and listening with empathy, we were able to get clarity and make a difference in their lives."

Mannino's screening strategy gave his department a clearer view of why certain adolescents kept getting in trouble, which led them to sustainable solutions. By actively seeking clarity, he and his teams helped alleviate an ongoing issue.

In an office setting, seeking clarity might look more like asking empathetic questions to suss out the source of an ongoing interpersonal conflict or coaxing more information out of an underperforming employee to find a root cause. Regardless of the circumstances, skipping this type of inves-tigation leaves leaders in the dark.

Now, if it's employees who are being left in the dark due to lack of clarity, another risk is that they will make assump-tions. In *The Good Culture*, Rebecca Friese wrote, "In the absence of information people will connect the dots in the most paranoid way possible... Clarity leads to alignment of values and, by extension, a focused purpose."

She's so right. Sometimes when business leaders are crystal clear, kind, and understanding, things still seem to go wrong. Even when met with honest and compassionate clarity, some people will still get upset, lash out, and quit. As leaders, that's not our fault.

By practicing clarity, we may unexpectedly find out that certain team members are simply in the wrong roles or even that they're no longer a values fit for our companies. That can be shocking, but it's not necessarily bad. Our clear commu-nication has helped us find a root cause for friction, which means we can address the issue head-on. Empathy becomes part of the equation when we take the time to walk them through that revelation, help them sort through their other options, and decide their next steps. And as leaders, we need to be okay with letting them go. Our people ultimately have to make their own decisions and decide what's best for their own careers. This can mean encouraging them to be decisive about what they really want, including recognizing if their role or the company are no longer aligned with their values or priorities.

In an article for LinkedIn, investor, board member, and former eBay CEO Maynard Webb responded to a mid-level manager's question about his company's return-to-work mandates and how he could get his leaders to change the policy. Webb put the responsibility for decision-making back on the manager to be clear on his own values, saying, "We are still in a state of flux so making sense of it, and making the best decisions, comes down to knowing the values and beliefs of the company and determining if that syncs with what you want to do. I know it may not feel this way, but you have to realize that you are in control. You may believe this is in someone else's hands, but it's in yours. You get to decide." (This also ties into the Decisiveness Pillar, which we'll explore together in the coming chapter.)

A caveat: I once knew someone who lacked tact and just said whatever she thought, whenever she thought it. Her excuse for hurting feelings and alienating others? "I'm just being honest."

Clarity and honesty are great, but we can engage in what they refer to at Gary Vaynerchuk's global advertising and media company VaynerMedia as "kind candor." To be clear and honest doesn't mean you have to be a jerk. Too many people mislabel harsh directness as empathetic truth telling. You can be clear in a kind, non-defensive, and, dare I say, non-preachy way that isn't dripping in smugness.

Researcher and author Brené Brown says, "Clear is kind. Unclear is unkind." I'm 100 percent with her. Even if it results in parting ways with an employee, sternly enforcing a boundary, or holding someone accountable, clarity is ultimately a form of compassion. And a vitally important one for empathetic leaders to learn and practice.

Building on this, we'll dive into the importance of decisiveness in the coming chapter and explore how acting in a clear, timely, and resolute manner is its own form of kindness.

Everyday Empathy Check-In: Clarity

- What can I get crystal clear on today? This week? This month? How have I communicated this and kept it front and center for the team?

- Does everyone on the team understand their own role in the purpose and mission and how their current workload contributes to it? Don't assume. Ask.

- Are we clear on how to best communicate and collaborate? If not, how can we document rules of engagement for current projects or everyday interactions so we can hold each other accountable and avoid misunderstanding?

- Am I avoiding a conversation or decision right now? If so, why? And what do I need to tackle it head-on?

For more prompts and free resources to help you practice clarity, please head to TheEmpathyDilemma.com/Resources.

Chapter Highlights

- Clarity is a crucial yet underrated aspect of leadership that is often neglected in practice.

- True clarity in leadership involves genuine and reciprocal communication, connecting it back to empathy and compassion.

- On the one hand, leaders who embrace clarity benefit from improved team performance, better boundary enforcement, and reduced risk of burnout, leading to a more positive work environment. On the other hand, lack of clarity can lead to demotivation, misunderstandings, and detrimental assumptions that may impact team dynamics and company culture.

- Practicing clarity in leadership fosters trust and loyalty among team members, reduces conflicts, and empowers employees to take ownership of their roles and responsibilities.

- Clarity should not be confused with harsh directness that hurts people. We can be clear *and* kind at the same time if we honor the impact our words can have on others around us.

DECISIVENESS

Build Trust, Gather Input, and Make the Call

"Dragging your heels on making a decision because you might offend someone isn't the same thing as being empathetic. You can be empathetic and be extremely decisive in the moment when you need to be."
KAT GORDON, social change entrepreneur and founder of the 3% Movement

What Is Decisiveness? Taking thoughtful but swift action that doesn't leave people hanging, addressing issues before they fester, synthesizing input and perspectives to make timely choices, and practicing radical and kind honesty.

Why Is Decisiveness Important? Keeping people in limbo is one of the least empathetic things a leader can do. It can feel risky to commit to decisions quickly, but dragging your feet to avoid hurt feelings will only erode trust. Addressing choices, performance issues, action plans, and pending questions as soon as possible is the most compassionate way to operate. Doing this shows your team members that you are paying attention and want them to know what to expect. It helps them fully understand what's happening around them. Decisiveness helps leaders maintain team momentum, cultivate trust, and build a culture of open and consistent honesty.

MOST EMPATHETIC leaders strive to hear and implement input from all their people. But sometimes endlessly soliciting everyone's feedback for unanimous agreement can drive your team mad.

Years ago, I worked with a brand client that made an innovative lifestyle consumer product. They had options to distribute it direct to consumers or to go through large retail partners. Both options had pros and cons, which meant the company was also considering pursuing both channels simultaneously.

I was hired to help them craft brand messaging to attract and engage the right audience. That discussion depended on which distribution model they chose as their primary one. Did they want to prioritize talking to direct consumers or to retail partners?

Mind you, I'm not a business model expert or operations consultant. I'm a brand messaging strategist. A client's business and distribution model should be fully baked and the primary audience determined (with the proper revenue analysis) before they begin crafting a high-level brand story to speak to said audience.

Everyone at all levels of this lifestyle product company had opinions, but what was crystal clear in the brand workshop was that the CEO's ongoing indecision on the distribution model priority was a source of pain. The leadership team had all weighed in multiple times on the pluses and minuses of each avenue, which was fantastic: everyone had their say. They knew they could find a way to make any model work within their various roles. What they needed was a final call on the primary distribution strategy so they could create their plans and take action.

But the CEO continued to ask what each of them thought, again and again, in the name of being collaborative and democratic. And his unwillingness to commit and lead on this important strategic point was wearing the whole team down. As one person admitted to me confidentially, "Could he just make a freaking decision already so we can *move*?!"

This CEO believed he was being empathetic by continually soliciting feedback and input. And that's understandable, given our definition: being willing and able to see, understand, and (where appropriate) feel another person's perspective, and to use that information to act compassionately. But the *leaderly* aspect of empathetic leadership requires knowing when you've gathered enough perspectives to forge ahead. It's not about trying to find a nonexistent path that will fully please everyone. In fact, the empathetic move on this leader's part would have been to thank his team for their perspectives, consider their input carefully but quickly trust himself to be decisive, and explain why he made the ultimate decision.

Patrick Morrissey, chief customer officer at HireVue, has witnessed the critical importance of decisiveness and the frustrations that arise when leaders are too hesitant to act.

> I know leaders who have been too slow to act where there was a problem because they wanted to think the best about people. I want to give them credit for their intent. People build up relationship credit over time. And then when something goes a little bit sideways, if you already have a positive relationship with them, you might look the other way. But that can't happen if you need to remove them from their position or fire them. If someone has either crossed the line or is no longer capable of doing the job, you need to act. You'll waste a lot of cycles for everybody—starting with yourself—if you don't move fast enough to make those changes.

Of course, taking swift, informed action can be easier said than done. Plenty of research has highlighted the issues of split attention and chronic stress affecting leaders' ability to act quickly and confidently. In a recent McKinsey survey, just over half of respondents reported spending more than 30 percent of their working time on decision-making, and more than 23 percent said they spent a majority of their time making decisions. The group polled included both leaders and employees, showing that everyone across workplace hierarchies is tasked with fielding tough choices. Another study of one thousand C-suite leaders from companies of more than five hundred employees found that these leaders spent between 40 and 100 percent of their time making decisions! Clearly, executives are overloaded with issues that require their brainpower and signoffs, a situation that causes stress levels to skyrocket.

And, it turns out, stress can become a vicious circle. Researchers have reported that decision-making can lead to stress and fatigue, and that chronic stress alters brain chemistry and leads to poor decision-making. So once leaders fall into the pattern, it can feel impossible to break free. The longer it goes on, the harder it becomes to make sound business choices. Remaining locked in a stress cycle is a recipe for burnout and the polar opposite of self-compassion.

Adding to that stressful pile-on? Indecisive leaders cost their companies a ton of money. According to that same McKinsey survey, "On average, respondents spend 37 percent of their time making decisions, and more than half of this time was thought to be spent ineffectively. For managers at an average Fortune 500 company, this could translate into more than 530,000 days of lost working time and roughly $250 million of wasted labor costs per year." Yikes.

Clearly, leaders who embrace decisiveness have everything to gain: more impact, less stress, higher productivity, and increased energy for other tasks. Not to mention more stability and trust for your team members. After all, empathetic decisiveness means soliciting other perspectives and points of view to see a clear picture, and *then* making a decision actively and swiftly. When team members see this in action, they feel valued and included. And these feelings carry over when leaderly decisiveness is funneled into the creation of boundaries, standard operating procedures, and other guardrails that make work flow more easily.

"Picking some non-negotiables early on—including a framework of rules to follow—and letting your team know is more empathetic than improvising all the time," said Jonni

Ressler, CEO of marketing consultancy Eleven 11 Solutions. "Because if you keep changing things on them, you're leaving them in a state of uncertainty, which isn't very empathetic."

Let's be clear: being empathetic does not give you an excuse to be indecisive or stop driving performance. This is why the Self-Care Pillar is so crucial: when you understand yourself and set your boundaries, you can be empathetic yet still focus on the goal. "It's my job to make this team run well, period," said chief marketing officer Tracy Eiler. "You need to be very good at putting on and off hats. I can have my empathy hat and leverage that so that we can have an open conversation, but I have a responsibility to the organization that we need to run it well." Eiler goes on to say that understanding that this is always her first priority helps her with her own emotional reaction to a situation and helps her push through to address situations in a timely manner. "We all know it's easy to use empathy as an excuse to not be direct, to not performance-manage someone. I really feel like one of the hardest things about being a leader is how you balance being empathetic and driving performance."

Indeed, that balance is harder for some more than others. Indecisive leaders also need to reflect on what their indecision is caused by: ability or avoidance? They may feel uncomfortable dealing with tough situations and turn to avoidance as a coping strategy. As leadership coach and author of *Chief Inspiration Officer* Val Ries shared with me in an interview, "They're avoiding difficult conversations, they're avoiding hurting someone's feelings, they're avoiding addressing something because it's awkward. Or they simply don't know how to redirect the conversation. In my view, lack of decisiveness is actually just avoiding saying the things you really want to say. Even though it can result in things just becoming a mess." Ries goes on to say that as such leaders uncomfortably witness others defending or arguing, they may just fall back on dictating a decision without thoughtful input, stating, "No, you need to do this" in order to ease their own stress and discomfort. Swinging the pendulum too far in either direction is never good.

No one does well when the rules of the game are constantly in flux. Being decisive as a leader is an effective (and underrated) way to demonstrate compassion for your people and yourself. Let's explore how else this pillar is beneficial.

How Does Decisiveness Benefit Empathetic Leaders?

If we're taking lessons on leadership decisiveness, one of the best workplaces to look at is a hospital. In the medical profession, lives are on the line if decisions remain unmade. I know this from personal experience.

At the age of thirty-five—and in the healthy, vibrant prime of my life—I had a ruptured brain aneurysm that nearly killed me. An ambulance had rushed me to the hospital, where emergency surgery saved my life.

I was in the hospital for six weeks, first in the neurological ICU and then in in-patient rehab. The slow work of recovery began. The cerebral rupture was so severe that it caused hemorrhaging in my retinas, resulting in temporary near blindness, which eventually resolved through interventional surgery and time.

The month of August 2008 is lost to me, save for a few snatches of memory here and there, like images remembered from a dream. Having lost my short-term memory temporarily, I didn't become fully aware of my surroundings until September, even though I was awake and talking to people. The University of Washington Medical Center was where I began the long process of reclaiming my life. Not only did the "brain ninjas" pull me back from the brink, but the care and compassion I received as a patient there impacted me deeply.

One of the healthcare professionals who has become a partner in my ongoing care and maintenance to ensure this doesn't happen again is neurosurgeon Dr. Robert Dodd. When I moved back to the San Francisco Bay Area from Seattle, I needed to find a new neurosurgeon to continue my ongoing scans and check-ins. I was referred to Dr. Dodd at Stanford Medicine, and he has been a godsend. He even performed a harrowing brain surgery on me in 2019, when it was time to clip a second aneurysm to proactively prevent it from rupturing and wreaking as much havoc as the first. This required a big decision on our part about which procedure to choose: the best option for me involved cutting open my skull, so, yeah, we had to weigh some risks.

These kinds of decisions require trust in knowing the expert understands what's important to you—and honestly, it wasn't hard to trust him: In every interaction we had with him, Dr. Dodd struck me as someone who has gravitas and compassion in equal parts. Like all neurosurgeons, he works in a very high-stress, high-stakes profession, so when I first decided to write this book, I knew I needed to ask him how he balances empathy with life-saving decision-making. And in his characteristically concise way, he boiled it down for me.

"My empathy is to always understand and put myself in the patients' and families' shoes no matter what difficult thing they're going through," Dr. Dodd said. "If it's a life-threatening situation, and I know that if I move forward, I'm going to save someone's life and they will be much happier in the end, then I have to assert myself and figure out a way to solve the problem. I'm not going to stop to have a touchy-feely conversation."

Decisiveness like that isn't just compassionate; it's vitally important in Dr. Dodd's line of work. If he were to prevaricate at all, he'd be doing his patients and their families a massive disservice. They don't need overwhelming options when someone's life is on the line; they need to trust the professional in charge. And when they feel comfortable doing that, they'll feel relief knowing they can trust him to do what needs to be done.

In an office setting, the stakes may be lower, but the benefits are just as numerous. Here are some ways that decisiveness supports empathetic leaders.

Decisiveness Shows Respect

To be blunt, waffling wastes everyone's time. While wise leaders will always weigh their options carefully, decisive leaders never allow themselves to get lost in the weeds. Stalling out of fear or indecision wastes your time and energy, as well as the time and energy of everyone involved in the choice you're not making. Since that means you're prioritizing your comfort over everyone else's needs, that amounts to disrespect. One way to frame this is to think about former U.S. secretary of state Colin Powell's 40/70 rule. He would never make a decision with less than 40 percent of the information he needed, but he would still feel fully confident with his choice, even when he had only 70 percent. The best leaders avoid tunnel vision or rash decisions by soliciting information and ideas from different perspectives first, to be sure, but are able to plow ahead when they have just the right amount of intel and certainty.

Decisiveness Relieves Stress

"The best leaders are able to be there for their teams and make tough decisions with compassion," said Amanda Carlson-Phillips, chief performance innovation officer at corporate well-being, professional development, and sport performance company Exos. "They don't respond with a short fuse. They don't say, 'Oh my gosh, I'm totally stressed and I don't have time to deal with your complaint.'" And as we discussed earlier in this chapter, decisive leaders are able to reduce their

The *leaderly* aspect of empathetic leadership requires knowing when you've gathered enough perspectives to forge ahead.

stress load—and that of their teams—by being efficient and effective whenever a choice presents itself.

Decisiveness Leads to Prioritization

On the one hand, when leaders are unable to make expedient choices, progress halts. Team members may not know where to focus their energies and end up working on the wrong projects. The leaders themselves may spend so much time trying to make the right call that they miss out on timely opportunities. Decisive leaders, on the other hand, are able to cut through the noise and set solid priorities for themselves and their people. Ann Latham, author and president of Uncommon Clarity, sees making quick but informed choices as central to effective leadership. "You could argue decision-making is absolutely the most important activity for any person in any organization," she said. "Because we make decisions all day long. And decisions unleash next steps. They are what constitute honest-to-goodness progress so that you can move other things forward."

Decisiveness Fosters Confidence

Modeling the ability to make informed decisions expediently and confidently is the best possible way to encourage your team members to do the same. Steve Hartman, chief customer officer at Rugs USA, is a proponent of leading by example when it comes to making business choices. "Being decisive and operating with a sense of urgency as a leader helps make sure other people feel enabled to make decisions fast, rather than feeling like they need to think through things to the umpteenth degree," he explained. And as someone who suffered under indecisive leaders who changed strategy every other day based on the last person they spoke to, I can attest that such leaders cause smart, motivated people to move forward half-heartedly in case they have to scrap it all and start again!

How to Incorporate More Decisiveness

Wondering how to hone your decisiveness as an empathetic leader? Here's how to get started.

"Too many people see empathy and decisiveness as mutually exclusive," psychologist Dr. Rebecca Eldredge said on an episode of my podcast. "'Either I'm really being empathetic and compassionate with my team members, or I'm making the business decisions that need to be made.' And I think these things are very much integrated. You're much more equipped to make solid decisions when you are in an empathetic and compassionate role, with your team members and also with yourself."

She makes it sound so simple. But does leading with decisive empathy sound easier said than done? If so, I get it. Many of us tend to associate decisiveness with the steely, no-nonsense, empathy-free leadership style of decades gone by. It smacks of business-first prioritization and valuing speed over measured consideration of options.

This is only true if you make decisions in a vacuum, with no input or perspective from anyone else. If you are a dictator who arrogantly thinks you are the only one with all the answers.

The art of empathetic decision-making encourages and honors other points of view to ensure you're not missing anything, as you swiftly make the best decision.

But as we've just learned, making quick-but-informed choices is far from cold and heartless when done with intention. Here's how to foster decisiveness in yourself and fold it into your leadership practice.

Revisit Your Goal and Purpose—Often

Much of the time, leaders can get caught up in the drama surrounding important decisions and lose sight of the goal. Create a way to clearly kick yourself in the pants as you make a decision: make your goal physically visible using a sticky note or by including it at the top of every discussion agenda. Read the mission out loud when you kick off meetings to reorient everyone to true north.

Here are some tactics to try:

- **Bake in goal-review processes:** Don't just trust yourself to remember. Create mechanisms that enable both you and your team members to keep purpose top of mind throughout the work. In addition to the suggestions above, you can add goal statements to tracking paperwork, insist on reviewing the purpose at every major goalpost, or ask stakeholders to consider the overall goal any time they request a change or addition.

- **Make goal-centricity a group endeavor:** Ask your team members or colleagues to be accountability partners to you in remaining goal-focused. Tell them you are training yourself to be more decisive and need their help. Then enlist them to ask you, "Which option aligns with the larger purpose?" whenever they see you waffling.

Practice Transparency

There's no need to make all decisions in a secretive way and unveil them only when they are fully baked. Learn to be clearer quicker, and if possible, talk openly about the choices you're making and have made. Say what you mean and mean what you say. Don't be afraid to say, "I don't know, but let's find out together." By intentionally creating a transparent culture, your people are more likely to provide valuable input you may have overlooked as well as trust your tough decisions because they know you have their backs.

Here are some tactics to try:

- **Share your failures:** I know, this is a painful one. But transparency isn't just about communication; it's about accountability and honesty. Being human with your teams means they'll feel comfortable doing the same. This builds empathy that runs in both directions. It also will slowly erode any anxiety you have about making "bad" or "wrong" decisions. Sharing faulty decisions openly helps you process them more fully, which equips you to avoid them in the future. And make better decisions faster!

- **Process with trusted colleagues:** Many leaders feel compelled to make decisions in isolation. It feels less risky and more leaderly somehow. But it also cuts those leaders off from potentially valuable outside perspectives and removes an avenue for transparency. By allowing yourself to verbally process with team members or other leaders, you reveal your thought processes and limiting factors.

Solicit and Synthesize Input Quickly and Fairly

Become skilled at gathering facts and opinions, giving others a voice so they can point out opportunities or risks you may have missed, sorting through all the inputs, and coming to a conclusion. Practice soliciting input from others, but be clear that once a decision is made, naysayers will be asked to disagree but commit. At a certain point, we've all got to move forward together and still be committed to the mission.
Here are some tactics to try:

- **Focus on impact:** General feedback is important, especially as an on-ramp to frequent and honest feedback, but if you want to be decisive by implementing input quickly, you need specifics. Ask the feedback-giver to recommend one thing you could do that would make a difference to them, specifically. Framing your request in this way can reveal issues at the core of your relationship. You can also make this ask after you've been given more overarching, general input to home in on specific actions you can take.

- **Express enthusiasm for feedback aloud:** Ideally, soliciting input should be constant, not sporadic. Remind your teams how much you value their perspectives and feedback at the beginning or end of each meeting. The more they hear about your openness, the more comfortable they'll become offering their honesty.

- **Start small:** Testing out feedback through small experiments lowers the stakes and potential costs of committing to a permanent shift in behavior or mindset. It also shows the person who has offered feedback that you take their opinion seriously. Here's a low-risk experiment to practice synthesizing and deciding quickly. Ask everyone to vote for the location of the next off-site, department lunch, or team-building activity. Then leverage all that input to quickly make a call yourself, as the leader. Finally, practice communicating your choice back to everyone, even if some of those people don't like the idea.

Put a Deadline on Your Thoughts

Decisiveness isn't only about making good choices; it's about making good choices *in a timely manner*. If you tend to ruminate endlessly, you need a mechanism to get yourself unstuck, such as setting aside a block of time to make a decision, which is itself a task. In an article for *Fast Company*, psychotherapist Amy Morin recommends getting in the habit of setting deadlines for decisions that trip you up. If it's a small decision—say, picking a spot for a business lunch—give yourself a few hours. If it's weightier—a big investment or strategic pivot—think more in terms of days or weeks.

Here are some tactics to try:

- **Leverage tech:** It may sound simple, but just putting a reminder in your phone or calendar can help you stay on track to make decisions in a timely manner. It'll feel annoying at first, but if it trains you to be more decisive overall, the initial irritation will be worthwhile.

- **Schedule a decision review block each day:** If decision-by-decision scheduling is too onerous, consider setting aside thirty minutes or so each day to review and mull upcoming choices. This is also a good forcing mechanism for leaders who are overwhelmed by choices.

Build Trust

In an environment where trust has been cultivated and built, people are more willing to trust a leader's decisions, even if it's a tough decision for them to swallow. If your people don't trust you, they're less likely to think your decisions have been reached fairly, with everyone's input and overall best interests in mind. This may not link directly to your own ability to make decisions as a leader, but it's vitally important to ensure those decisions are accepted, instead of questioned and picked apart.

Remember the financial services client that I mentioned back in the introduction? In the aftermath of the COVID pandemic, I advised the department leaders who were struggling to convince some people on their teams to return to the office. Like many people, the members of this team had grown accustomed to working remotely and were frustrated that their colleagues in other roles could still do some of their work from home. The company's leadership wanted to handle this issue as empathetically as possible but also firmly believed that it was optimal for the business (and for legal requirements) if employees in certain roles were all working together in person. And as I said in the introduction, I ended up telling them that their issue wasn't empathy: *it was trust.* The staff were resistant because they didn't trust that leadership was making decisions with their best interests in mind.

Leaders who embrace
decisiveness have
everything to gain:
more impact, less stress,
higher productivity,
and increased energy
for other tasks.

Perhaps this foundation of trust was shaky from before the pandemic hit, or else the team might have returned to the office without resistance. The decision that leadership handed down might have been accepted expediently, enabling leaders to move quickly to the next important choice that needed making.

Remember, trust always runs in both directions. Technology CEO and growth leader Guy Weismantel told me, "As a leader, you need to leave your ego behind when you don't know the answer. Whether the question comes from a staff member or a board member, you've got to be able to say, 'That's a great question. I don't have that information, but I can get it for you by this time tomorrow.' Versus leaders who are like, 'Oh, yes, I know everything we need to know. Or I'm at least going to pretend I do.'"

Weismantel added, "There is a short fuse right now around job performance, achieving success, and hitting metrics for CEOs and the board of directors. So when things go wrong, it's really easy for leaders to just want to grab control themselves and own the problem. But I think, ultimately, that's shortsighted. It's just like a sugar rush. It can't last forever. And in the end, it erodes your team members' trust in you when things really get tough."

Here are some tactics to try:

- **Follow through on your promises:** Trust is about stability and predictability. When team members repeatedly see that your words and actions are in sync, it eases their anxieties. They will believe that when you say you'll commit to a path, you'll actually do it. That can shore up trust in other areas over time too.

- **Be honest:** Many of the recommendations and tactics in this section connect or ladder up to each other, and building trust is no different. Being honest and transparent with your team members and colleagues—including sharing failures and processing out loud—will help create a trusting environment.

- **Avoid micromanagement:** Trust flows both ways and showing your team members that you trust them helps them learn to trust *you*. Set clear expectations and keep communication flowing, but don't hover or meddle where you're not needed. If the work gets done and the goals are met, everything is fine. Instead, offer yourself as a standing resource that people can seek out when they realize they need support. If you can't trust your people, perhaps you hired the wrong people or have your own internal control issues you need to examine. For Pete's sake, stop with the badge swipes and keystroke tracking! It's just inhumane.

Adopt a Design-Thinking Approach

Design thinking asks us to experiment and try things out to see if they will fly in the real world. If you force yourself to consider every option until you're sure you've selected the "perfect" one, you may never make a decision for fear of being wrong. Perfection isn't the goal, even when it comes to high-stakes choices. Don't succumb to analysis paralysis. Instead, gather input, decide, and move forward with a sense of curiosity and experimentation.

Here are some tactics to try:

- **Trust yourself to adapt:** As a leader, the choices you make will impact others. So by no means should you take them lightly or ignore the practice of due diligence. But you'll move toward a more decisive style of leadership if you know you're capable of adapting, pivoting, or reconfiguring processes should you ever choose incorrectly. It's also more collaborative if your team knows you're willing to adapt when new information presents itself.

- **Create CO-STORMING™ sessions:** Melody Biringer is the founder of Women in Tech Regatta, which hosts events in different cities to elevate women in the tech industry and connect them with mentors and resources. At many of these events Biringer organizes CO-STORMs™, where people bring their ideas to a group to get "fresh eyes" and "see our blind spots and filters." To do this in your own company, gather a diverse group and allow people to poke holes in assumptions, offer "what if?" scenarios, and even play devil's advocate. By questioning norms and thinking differently, you can experiment with new ways to solve tough challenges.

I'm going to risk looking a bit stodgy by including a quote from a long-dead American president here. Theodore Roosevelt—a bold and effective decision-maker if ever there was one—is credited with saying, "In any moment of decision, the best thing you can do is the right thing, the next best thing is the wrong thing, and the worst thing you can do is nothing." I can honestly say that I think this advice applies to the modern empathetic workplace. Leaving people hanging erodes trust and wastes resources. Choosing confidently and communicating your choices helps your team understand what's happening around them and make informed decisions of their own.

As Empathy Activist, author of the award-winning book *Tell Me More about That*, and founder of consumer insights research firm Ignite 360 Rob Volpe said, "Empathy is what you're going to apply in the communication so that the employee hears the decision and, at least, feels recognized and heard."

Absolutely true… but some leaders still conflate sugar-coating and delaying bad news with empathy. If you're a chronic waffler or an indirect communicator, what challenges will that bring?

What You Risk If You Don't Embrace Decisiveness

Making sure to address issues before they fester, synthesizing input to make quick choices, and practicing radical transparency all help leaders create a culture of trust. But what happens if leaders just... don't do those things? What are the results of indecisive leadership?

Let's look at how some leaders in fields where lives are on the line deal with balancing empathy with decisiveness.

A warning: The following story talks about decisiveness in a life-or-death situation where painful choices must be made to save lives. It's meant to show how decisiveness is required in times of crisis to benefit the greater good. It may be triggering for anyone who has experienced gun violence; feel free to skip ahead to the next section, "When It's Time to Part Ways."

Retired police chief Christopher Mannino's perspective sheds a sober light on the importance of making quick and wise leadership decisions. He talks about his training for active shooter and active threat events, and the prioritization that goes along with them.

"In these trainings, we're taught to move past victims and go to the person causing the threat," he explained. "If you're an empathetic person, that can feel hard. You're passing up people who need your help right now, but you're doing it to prevent more people from becoming victims."

Mannino points out that part of being a leader in a crisis means keeping the bigger, more urgent priority in mind. People may feel confused or slighted in the moment, but they'll understand your deep-rooted empathy once the danger has passed.

"You're placing a priority on what must be done," he said. "It doesn't mean you don't care; it just means you recognize that, at this point, the mission is the most critical aspect. And really, it's probably the most empathetic thing you can do. Because you're stopping the threat as quickly as possible."

Former emergency room registered nurse and now nurse innovator and public speaker Rhonda Manns echoed this philosophy in an interview: "As hard as it is, you learn how to treat the case and nurture the person." She went on to talk about how both are possible at the same time. "As a first responder, I wasn't enmeshed and all gooey about everything in the moment. I was good at my job, and people felt very cared for because when I was present, I was present. You can safely have the psychological distance to perform your job well and not get sucked into the nuances of how terrible this case is."

Now, I know that relatively few of you are working in environments where lives are literally on the line. But this philosophy applies to all kinds of situations where there is chaos and uncertainty.

It's so easy to think of empathy as the accumulation of small acts of kindness over days, weeks, and months. And sometimes it is! But if all of those kindnesses are just distractions from a hard decision or change that needs to be addressed—layoffs, termination of a project, changing a popular policy, a demotion—the truly empathetic choice would be to take thoughtful but swift action.

As Mannino's example illustrates, leaders who lack decisiveness risk eroding trust, skewing priorities, and prioritizing their own comfort over taking tough but compassionate action. Empathetic leadership isn't always about making people feel warm and fuzzy inside; often, it's about doing what will best support their growth, balancing their needs with business priorities, or being extremely candid instead of prolonging an unhealthy situation.

When It's Time to Part Ways

This sentiment that empathetic leadership is not just about the warm fuzzies, but being kindly candid rather than prolong a bad situation, can even extend to transferring or letting people go. If, as a leader, you've done everything in your power to meet someone's needs but you've reached an impasse, being decisive about letting them go can be the most compassionate choice. Especially if their demands contradict business needs or important policies. In researching this book, I spoke with multiple leaders across many industries who agreed that sometimes you must reexamine someone's job description with them, remind them what they signed up to do, and have an honest discussion about that. You may want to say something like, "If this isn't a good fit for you anymore, I understand. Our lives and circumstances change. Maybe this is no longer the right role for you, but this is what the company requires. The organization needs you to fulfill these duties, and if that's no longer aligned with your needs, I can help you look at other options."

It sounds scary, and in the moment it probably will be. But many of the leaders who advocated for this kind of decisiveness also told me that many of their people recognize its importance in the moment or soon afterward.

"So often, I've had folks just thank me when I have fired them for performance," said author Tracy Eiler. "They have thanked me for helping them see that something wasn't a fit, so that they could go find the thing that was."

Guy Weismantel echoed this sentiment:

> You can be super empathetic and tell someone on your team, "Look, your performance is slipping and here's where I'm seeing it show up. If you don't feel you're in a good place right now to be able to participate fully to achieve our goals, I totally get it. We all go through different seasons; we all have different things going on. And I don't want to diminish

what you're going through. But it just may be that you're not in the right spot right now to help us get to where we need to. What do you think? Is this how you're seeing things or do you have a different view of what's going on?" Those are the times I'm trying to be empathetic while also staying accountable to the other people that are depending on me to get their bonus and deliver on their work.

Thankfully, empathetic leadership isn't all tough decisions and compassionate layoffs. In the coming chapter, we'll talk about cultivating something that's frequently overlooked in working environments but crucial to ensuring both leaders and team members remain engaged and connected: joy.

Everyday Empathy Check-In: Decisiveness

- Is there a call that needs to be made today? What can I decide today rather than put off to tomorrow? If I am procrastinating, dig deep and ask why. What do I need to move forward?

- Do we, as a team, vet choices against a clear and actionable purpose and values so we can make better, faster decisions? If not, why not?

- Have I solicited feedback from people with different perspectives and experiences, who may see the challenge in a new way or identify unseen risks and opportunities? Has everyone been heard?

- How can I more quickly synthesize various perspectives and then move forward with a sound decision? What gets in my way? Why do I never think I have enough information to move forward in a way everyone trusts?

For more prompts and free resources to help you balance empathy and decisiveness, please head to TheEmpathy Dilemma.com/Resources.

Chapter Highlights

- Embrace the practice of making decisions in a timely manner while considering the impact on others' time and understanding their perspectives. Aim to address issues promptly to avoid leaving people in uncertainty.

- While seeking input is important, avoid getting stuck in the pursuit of unanimous agreement or satisfaction. Strive to strike a balance between gathering insights and making timely choices.

- Recognize the impact of chronic indecision on stress levels and overall decision-making quality. Aim to make well-informed decisions efficiently to reduce stress and set clear priorities.

- Foster a culture of trust by openly communicating decisions and their underlying reasons. Share both successes and failures and involve the team in decision-making processes.

- Understand that decisiveness can sometimes mean prioritizing the larger goal or mission over individual preferences. Recognize that tough decisions can ultimately lead to a more empathetic and supportive environment.

8

JOY

How Canned Fish Mondays
and Zoom Goats Foster Connection

*"Leaders who intentionally build in those extra
minutes in meetings to hear people out, offer comfort or
advice, and even leave space for laughter and occasional
nonsense are ultimately building a more resilient team."*
JOHN JACOBS, cofounder and
chief creative optimist of Life Is Good

What Is Joy? Ensuring people enjoy their work, encouraging work friendships, and creating a thriving culture even when the work itself is challenging.

Why Is Joy Important? Multiple studies have shown that when people enjoy their work it leads to lower rates of turnover, higher productivity and engagement, increased company profits, and loyalty to the employer. But beyond these pragmatic reasons, empathetic business leaders generally want their teams to be happy, successful, and fulfilled to buoy the overall culture. A joyful work culture breeds trust to collaborate, innovate, and take risks. It empowers people to have each other's backs.

WHEN WAS the last time you felt a sense of joy at work?

I don't just mean polite laughter at an all-hands meeting or gratitude for a well-timed delivery of leftover cake to the breakroom. Think about the last time you felt exhilarated when you completed a project, or genuinely excited to dive into a cross-functional partnership. How about the last time you had a friendship with a work colleague who supported and understood you so thoroughly they made every day more enjoyable?

Our current workplace paradigms and power structures can make these experiences rare. Organizations say they want more trust, innovation, and collaboration, but they aren't willing to be open-minded about how to foster those behaviors within their walls.

Jyoti Jani and Emily Griffin recognized this and decided to take matters into their own hands. Jani is the founder of Spille:Play, and as a coach and facilitator, she guides world-class technology and social impact teams to develop courageous leadership, craft inclusive cultures, and align to bold visions. Griffin is a multidimensional producer with roots in broadcasting, publishing, and DJing who's led global creative teams in technology, art, and entertainment for more than twenty years.

In the fall of 2020, these two powerhouses joined forces to create the Empathy Tour: they spent several months interviewing all types of leaders—both traditional ones and those underrepresented in the business world—to find out how they led, what challenges they faced, and the very real ways they were having impact and success through empathy. Through their consulting work, both Jani and Griffin had seen how painful it was for leaders and employees to work under the pressures of a "growth at any cost" mindset and wanted to help catalyze a shift. And they wanted to do it in a creative, joyful, playful way that would still yield outstanding results.

"We recognized that all of us are playful creatures, but at some point, as we grow up into this culture, we are taught that play is inappropriate, and that it's separate from work," Jani explained on an episode of *The Empathy Edge* podcast. "I had woven a lot of playful facilitation and methods into my own work and seen how play really opens up the team process. It opens up the human element; it makes empathy and creativity central to a team facilitation process rather than on the side. Ultimately, you end up with results that folks can really get on board with."

Throughout the Empathy Tour, Jani and Griffin offered up a guidebook with twenty-eight self-reflection prompts and team activities that their interviewees could use to explore empathy and encourage play in their own workplaces. They spent most of 2020 immersed in this work, undertaking it all amid the global pandemic. By the year's end, they'd concluded that the combination of play, accountability, and empathy is a truly powerful one, especially when we're faced with new challenges and levels of uncertainty.

"We asked, 'What are the barriers to us doing our best work together?' And most of the time, it's fear of judgment, fear of failure, fear of being seen in our truth," Jani said. "Play helps us release those fears."

She went on to describe an experience facilitating a roundtable of Lego® Serious Play with executives and engineers at the end of a two-day retreat. She saw folks who had been nearly silent for the entire retreat open up like blooming flowers when offered a play exercise. The joy they felt at experiencing empathy and creativity alongside their colleagues enabled them to engage at a whole new level.

"That's what we're really trying to do. We're trying to get each and every voice in the room, in the team, and in the organization contributing and speaking up," Jani said. "And play allows us to do that."

Of course, play isn't the only way to inject joy into your leadership practice.

When I first start working with any new client, I try to get a sense of the mood and temperament of the team. If it feels like everyone is just marinating in tense energy, my first inclination to create trust is to crack a joke. I like to lighten the mood or be a little playful with people to give them permission to let their guard down. And believe me, it works wonders. I can almost see this giant, shared exhalation of relief when they realize I'm not going to be some rigid taskmaster with a nine-hundred-slide deck of torture. Introducing the tiniest bit of joy at the beginning of my process is a long-standing strategy and one that helps me build rapport, encourage honesty, and ultimately unleash the best ideas.

It's worth noting, however, that joy can't be forced. And it certainly can't be bought.

We've all heard the tales of Silicon Valley offices chock-full of Ping-Pong tables, espresso machines, and... abject corporate misery. A set of brightly colored couches and kitchen full of free snacks does not a joyful company make. Sure, perks can help people feel appreciated, but not if they're more bribery than empathy. Perks are far less important than meaningful work, genuine demonstrations of appreciation and inclusion, and shared fun with trusted coworkers.

Workplace crusader and culture expert Rebecca Friese, cofounder of FLYN Consulting and author of *The Good Culture*, calls this surface attempt at building a joyful culture through perks rather than substantive connection "fungineering." Oh, if only it were that easy!

That said, when joy is done right, it can make a massive difference to a company's culture and success. Bob Nelson, coauthor of *Work Made Fun Gets Done!*, examined the publicly available variables that Great Place to Work uses to measure and rank its annual 100 Best Companies to Work For list (which is published by *Fortune*). Of those, he found that "81 percent of employees at companies ranked as 'great' [by Great Place to Work] described their office environments as fun. At companies that applied for inclusion—but didn't make the list—only 62 percent of employees did the same. This 19-point gap was one of the largest distinctions we found, reiterating previous research that suggests 'fun' is essential to a great work culture." And a 2022 study of nearly thirteen thousand global employees found that 27 percent of someone's overall life happiness can be explained by their happiness at work. Which means that cultivating joy at work can also support the Self-Care Pillar!

But most companies aren't prioritizing joy as a supporting pillar of workplace empathy. Research firm Kearney has been tracking joy at work since 2018 and notes that the "joy gap" is growing. The company reported, "In our 2021 survey, 61 percent of people felt less joy at work than they expected. That's an 8-point increase from 2018, when 53 percent of people felt less joy than expected."

Clearly, organizations could be doing more to foster joyful environments. And they should, since there's a positive correlation between how much fun people have at work and how socially accepting, ethical, and altruistic they act toward their colleagues. But beyond a supportive and enjoyable environment, how can cultivating joy help bolster your individual ability to lead with empathy?

How Does Joy Benefit Empathetic Leaders?

Years ago when I worked for Business Objects, a business intelligence software company now part of SAP, I comanaged a global roadshow for an important merger and product integration. We traveled to nearly eighty cities over the course of a six-week period, and I was responsible for leading the global effort, as well as managing the North American rollout. Believe me, I did not do this alone, but I had a big responsibility. Coordinating content from various people in field and product marketing. Assigning people to lead logistics, venue booking, and the event production company. Staffing speakers at concurrent events. Tracking the travel schedules of multiple colleagues. There were so many moving parts, and I had never managed anything this complex before. It had the makings of a multi-week nightmare.

But our team of field and product marketers and salespeople, collaborating together, knew exactly how to keep the roadshow from dragging us all down into a pit of despair.

The speakers who were traveling the circuit constantly sent back email reports of the unpredictable and often hilarious antics they'd witnessed at their events. Fire alarms going off mid-presentation. Harrowing tales of missed flights due to snowstorms and folks renting cars to drive from city to city in the freeze of Midwestern winter instead. Plus the global offices customized their events based on their cultural preferences, which meant that even aside from unplanned mayhem, the events were lively and engaging for both our employees and attendees. We got one report from a group staffing a European city—I can't even remember which one—but they did some wild parody of a rock show onstage. It was super weird and hilarious. While we all can't recall the exact details, we do all remember how enjoyable that moment was in the midst of this grueling schedule!

As a project leader in charge of this huge endeavor with dozens of moving parts (and since this was a temporary project team, no real authority over any of these folks), it helped me immeasurably to partner with a team that knew how to keep the mood light. I felt less stress and guilt over packing their schedules to the brim and sending them to far-flung cities, and those six weeks felt less onerous for us all with everyone cheering each other on. Knowing that they'd make the most of the roadshow and share laughs with everyone back at the office encouraged me to do everything in my power to build a painless travel experience for them. Without those bursts of joy between us colleagues, I might have been seen as the villain orchestrating their torture. I might have taken less care with their schedules. Heck, I might have even burned out from the intensity of the process.

Decades later, we all still fondly remember this experience.

Joy, fun, play, and humor can really transform how teams collaborate and how they feel about their work. These strategies aren't optional; they're crucial tools in the empathetic leader's toolbox. And they really do make your job easier as well as more enjoyable.

"There are a number of benefits to incorporating play into the working environment," said Jyoti Jani. "One is being able to hear from every voice in the room and use platform methods to make it more inviting for people to speak up. Play lowers the barrier. It's an amazing way to enhance psychological safety. Another benefit is when you create a playful set of boundary conditions for a team, it gives them permission to think more creatively and to make connections they wouldn't usually make."

She's so right. And here are three more ways that building a fun, joy-filled work environment can support you as a leader.

Joy Reduces Stress

Multiple studies have shown that experiencing joy or other positive emotions can help protect us from burnout or even recover from burnout. Sophie Cliff, known as the Joyful Coach, points out that experiencing positive emotions helps us build resilience, fortitude, and other qualities that help us to better manage stress. She explains the link through the broaden-and-build theory.

"According to prominent social psychologist Barbara Fredrickson, while negative emotions can prompt us to employ narrow, survival-oriented behaviors (such as engaging the fight/flight/freeze response), positive thoughts and emotions broaden our awareness and encourage new thoughts and actions," Cliff wrote. "Her broaden-and-build theory explains how when we experience positive emotions such as joy, we broaden our thinking and improve our cognitive functioning, allowing us to draw on a wide range of possible solutions and behaviors, therefore building a whole host of mental resources (including resilience) that help us to live enhanced, healthier, and more fulfilling lives."

Sounds amazing, right? Especially for leaders who are feeling the pinch of remaining empathetic during dynamic and trying times.

Happy Team Members Are Easier to Lead

Here's the basic equation: a workplace that lacks joy is likely to have employees who aren't thrilled about doing their work every day. Believe me, I've been there. I've worked in one or two environments reminiscent of the drab, soul-sucking workplace portrayed in the movie *Office Space*. Unhappy employees—even mildly unhappy ones—may resist feedback or gripe about their duties. Conflicts can arise more often, and special projects can become impossible to navigate when people are disengaged.

A team that shares joyful experiences is more likely to be flexible, cooperative, and open to input. Team members who have forged work friendships and enjoy their work are just plain easier to lead—which means that leaders who prioritize joy are making their own lives easier.

Fun Environments Foster Trust and Collaboration

I hinted at this earlier in the chapter, but want to emphasize it again. Joy isn't only about creating bursts of enjoyment for leaders and team members; it's a tool for building trust. When people become used to working in an environment that welcomes play and encourages fun, they feel comfortable being themselves. They trust themselves and they trust their colleagues, which enables them to collaborate more fully and creatively.

Cultivating joy isn't about creating the world's funniest workplace. It's about creating a workplace where people can relax.

Speaker, strategist, ex-tech leader, and comedian (stand-up and improv) Kathy Klotz-Guest preaches the gospel of joy as a trust-builder to her clients. She combines her business and comedy backgrounds to help leaders, teams, and brands be more creative and innovative through everyday joy. It's also the subject of her book *Stop Boring Me!*. Klotz-Guest told me, "If we can take some of the things that make improv teams so special and put that into business teams, we would trust each other more. Everybody wants big, crazy ideas, and yet we don't make it safe most of the time. Most cultures struggle to make people feel safe and capable of spitballing."

As an empathetic leader, fostering joy in your workplace will reduce your stress levels, make your leadership duties easier, and build trust between you and your team members. All fantastic benefits... but joy is such an ephemeral thing. So how do you integrate more joy into your daily tasks?

How to Incorporate More Joy

Joy may be fleeting, but it can also be fantastically simple to weave into your workplace. Even if your team works in a distributed or hybrid model. Professional meeting facilitator Jackie Colburn offered up this slightly off-kilter but unquestionably hilarious icebreaker to inject fun into video meetings: When you're leading a virtual workshop among team members of the same title/level, ask them, "What are you wearing on your feet?" Then ask them to show the group if they are comfortable doing so!

"I know this one is kind of goofy, but bear with me. I especially like using the prompt for virtual workshops because this detail is usually a mystery when dialing in from home," Colburn wrote. "That said, the last thing I want to do is make a junior-level employee feel awkward about sharing their footwear in front of a VP (and vice versa), so I only employ it when I'm working with a group that already has a good rapport and consists of team members who have similar titles/levels. It's a fun and lighthearted way to kick off the workshop with humor and playfulness."

Ready for some other ways to bring joy to your team? Let's dive in.

Find and Encourage Humor

The ability to laugh at ourselves and to find humor in tough situations is a sure sign of resilience, which is just what healthy teams need. Things can and will go wrong, but when we stop taking ourselves so seriously, we can engage our prefrontal cortex to problem-solve more effectively. (Plus, research shows that leaders with a sense of humor are viewed as 27 percent more motivating and admired than those who play it serious all the time.)

Humor doesn't need to be cracking jokes at the morning check-in meeting or performing skits at the all-hands gathering. First off, I know that both of those formats can make people nervous: some worry about causing offense, and others worry their material may fall flat in front of their colleagues. No one wants to be awkward branch manager Michael Scott from *The Office* on a regular basis. Luckily, encouraging humor can be far less formal and scripted. It includes things like sharing memes or web comics, asking trivia questions, or giving yourself a theme song and playing it on your phone whenever you enter a room. It can also be as simple as relating a mishap from a recent travel experience or (gently) poking fun at yourself for a recent mistake.

Patrick Morrissey, chief customer officer at HireVue, suggests relying on some of the humor that organically pops up in everyday modern life. "One great way to bring joy to the office or joy to a Zoom call is to get the kids and the dog involved," he said. "That's always *way* more interesting than whatever somebody's presenting on PowerPoint. Get a kid on screen and everyone is asking, 'Who is that little human? And what's her name and height and age?' Maybe she's got cake on her face, or the dog just wants to jump up and be petted. It lightens the mood and lets everyone laugh easily."

But a warning: most of this will all fall flat if there is no underlying trust.

Michelle Sherman, executive leadership coach and founder of VAST Institute, puts it this way: "In order for there to be joy, there needs to be imagination. In order for there to be imagination, there needs to be psychological safety. In order for there to be psychological safety, you need to create respect, trustworthiness and mutual benefit."

I agree wholeheartedly. Without those basic elements, no amount of team shenanigans will cover up the foundational cracks in your culture that not only prevent empathy but innovation and collaboration along with it.

Here are some tactics to try:

- **Use the rule of three:** This classic comedy formula involves listing out three related things and making sure the last item is an unexpected one. So if you're on a video meeting, you might say, "I miss so many things about working in person at the office: brainstorming in the conference room, swapping ideas over the cube walls, and wearing anything besides pajama pants."

- **Incorporate challenges and contests:** Big caveat for this one—do it sparingly and only if it meshes with your company culture. If you work in a very straitlaced environment, don't make your team participate in a marshmallow-eating competition. But if you're at a company that truly wants its people to have more fun, float the idea of a "cutest baby picture" contest or "most groan-worthy dad joke" challenge.

- **Don't try too hard:** Forcing yourself to clown never goes well—and isn't really the point of bringing humor into the workplace. "It's about being more generous with your laughter. It's about naming truths in our lives and giving a window into our humanity," said executive coach and *Humor, Seriously* coauthor Naomi Bagdonas. Dick Costolo, former CEO of Twitter, agrees: "The easiest way to be funny is not to try—instead, just look for moments to laugh."

Learn Improv Skills to Nurture Creativity and Trust

As a big-time theater geek myself, I was super excited to have Kathy Klotz-Guest on *The Empathy Edge* podcast. Before she began consulting, she led successful tech teams for seventeen years and trained at ComedySportz, L.A.'s Second City, and other places, so she's serious about humor! Klotz-Guest, Founder of Keeping it Human℠, recognized that improv best practices could be helpful to collaborative teams in virtually any environment and has since been teaching workplace teams how to use comedy and improv as tools to unleash trust and collaboration that leads to innovation.

"A lot of what I do is facilitating conversation, facilitating what's working and what's not," she explained. "The first thing is training their brains to think collaboratively. Now, everything in improv is about trust. If I don't trust the people I play with, I can't go out and do a good show, right? Collaborators have to be able to pass the ball to each other, and also understand what to do when they *get* a ball."

"It's about respecting ideas," said Klotz-Guest. "If I come up with an idea and somebody says, 'That's not going to work,' that shuts everything down. We need to learn better communication skills, how to collaborate, how to build on each other's ideas, and how to pass the ball."

Here are some tactics to try:

- **Practice "yes, and":** The central tenet of improv is to never shut someone else down; always add on to what they've said. In her book *Bossypants*, Tina Fey points out that "Here we are in Spain, Dracula" may be a tough setup, but if you say, "That's not where we are," the whole scene falls to pieces. Take whatever your partner hands you and build on it. In an office setting, this translates into reacting collaboratively, not as an adversary. I also term this "enriching" what someone has offered.

- **Listen intently:** Related to "yes, and" is the ability to listen and hear what others are saying to you. Far too many people listen shallowly while waiting for their turn to speak; that's not collaborative and it's certainly not empathetic. Actively listening to understand enables colleagues to better support each other. As Klotz-Guest said, "Start listening, listening, listening, listening. If somebody doesn't get it, if somebody makes a mistake—and there aren't any big mistakes in improv—listening will enable you to help them by adding on, no matter what. And mistakes in improv are gifts."

Encourage Workplace Friendships

The average person spends 81,396 hours—the equivalent of more than nine years—at work. And mountains of research indicate that having friends in the workplace doesn't only boost job satisfaction and performance, it also improves wellness. It's linked to a lower risk of burnout, improved mental health, and maybe even a longer life span, according to studies conducted across Europe and Israel.

As a leader, it's your role to foster a culture of warmth and connection so your team members know that work friendships are encouraged. "You need leaders to say being personal with each other is valuable, it matters, and it starts at the top," said Dr. Robert Waldinger, a professor of psychiatry at Harvard Medical School. "When that happens, the culture can shift in a company where people tend to know each other better, and then care about each other and care about the workplace."

And that divide between knowing and caring is an important one. When speaker, social relationships expert, and author of *The Business of Friendship* Shasta Nelson appeared on my podcast, she explained that work friendships are actually different than just being "friendly" at work.

"In a workplace, everybody should at least be at the bottom of the spectrum where they're friendly with each other, can rely on each other, are kind with each other, and are respectful to each other. That's the minimum," she said. "Then as you move up that spectrum, workplace friendships should be about halfway up. That means we can rely on each other, we trust each other, we have psychological safety. We feel like we can brainstorm and we're not going to be ridiculed or ostracized. We can admit we've got too much going on."

Here are some tactics to try:

- **Create a safe environment:** Building friendships is a socially vulnerable endeavor. No one will even attempt it if they are too worried about being reprimanded for getting off track or wasting time. As an empathetic leader, you can intentionally cultivate an environment where people feel comfortable being vulnerable, sharing their experiences, and building relationships. This can be as simple as encouraging your team members to go have coffee together or share details about their hobbies or lives outside work.

- **Be curious:** Most people decorate their offices or cubicles. One of the easiest ways to learn more about someone is to ask about a photograph, piece of art, comic, or object they've got in their space. Feeling disconnected at work? Use your natural curiosity to strike up a conversation. Especially if you see an indicator of a common interest. See eye-catching artwork on the wall behind someone's desk, or a cool knickknack on a shelf in every Zoom call? Ask about it! And encourage your team members to do the same.

- **Try the buddy system:** To be clear, no leader should force longtime employees to pair up. But assigning buddies or mentors to new hires can help them figure out where to find supplies and what the unwritten rules are, along with helping them connect with other people in the company. Hopefully, some buddies will eventually become friends.

Make Meaningful Team-Building a Priority

"I have always appreciated the efforts that went into team-building and trying to seek to understand people," said Patrick Morrissey. "Sometimes the exercises you have to go through are kind of hokey, but there's no substitute for spending time with people and really trying to understand a little more deeply who they are, how they behave, what they care about, and what motivates them. That allows you to have some insights into leading, coaching, and empowering people to get the best out of them."

He's so right. Team-building has gotten a bad rap over the years as a cheesy, forced way to forge bonds, but when it's done thoughtfully, it can totally transform interpersonal dynamics for the better. On *The Empathy Edge* podcast, I interviewed Teri Schmidt, CEO of Stronger to Serve Coaching & Teambuilding, and I found her model to be incredibly thoughtful. Her company facilitates Learn by Doing (Good) experiences: your team picks a specific interpersonal skill to master, and her experts coordinate all the details and then guide you through tailored education and self-exploration. Then you get to put those skills into action through a community service project of your choice, anything from supporting kids in low-income schools to providing comfort to the unhoused. Done like that, team-building can not only lead to the formation of work friendships and bolster trust among teammates, it can help everyone build important interpersonal skills, which ultimately creates a more connected team.

When I worked at an ad agency years ago, I organized participation in the United Way Day of Giving. We all spent an entire Saturday together, painting a domestic violence shelter. It gave our team a way to connect outside of the work we were doing, get involved in the community, get to know people who were different from us, and expand our thinking. (And our president almost got injured by a run-in with a paint can and a ladder. But that's another story.)

Before you pursue team-building, make sure that your internal culture is already serving the needs of your people. You're never going to solve bonding issues through manufactured events that nobody wants to attend. Team-building should be a source of shared joy, not a bandage slapped onto a festering cultural issue.

Here are some tactics to try:

- **Tie team-building to purpose:** If your company's mission is related to improving health outcomes, create a team-building endeavor that involves providing healthy snacks or enjoyable exercise to those in need. If your purpose is related to greening the environment or democratizing technology, find a team-building activity that aligns.

- **Give back to the community:** Just as Schmidt does, you can focus team-building on volunteering as a way to build shared empathy for the people you're serving.

Team-building should be a source of shared joy, not a bandage slapped onto a festering cultural issue.

- **Consider diverse needs:** Are you thinking of planning a happy hour even though you have a team member who is in recovery? Planning to go bowling despite several team members dealing with physical challenges? Be inclusive and intentional when you plan team-building activities and ensure you offer a variety of options that are accessible to everyone.

Celebrate Together

Joy at work is directly tied to feelings of purpose, accomplishment, and connection. That domino effect boosts engagement and, ultimately, performance. Which means that actively celebrating wins as a team will up the joy quotient faster than just about anything else. Naturally, this can mean bringing in doughnuts when the sales team closes a big deal, but it should also extend to individual accomplishments and small-group goals. Learn to celebrate progress *along the way*. If one of your project managers has finished up a particularly onerous product launch, give her a trophy during a team meeting and play "Eye of the Tiger" as she enters the room. If your department's administrative team has gone above and beyond, compose and record a song in their honor!

A recent study found that 37 percent of polled employees want to do better work when they receive personal recognition. And Great Place to Work's analysis of 1.7 million employee survey responses revealed that people who feel recognized are more than twice as likely to bring new ideas and innovation forward, compared to those who don't feel recognized. So find creative ways to lift each other up and show appreciation.

Here are some tactics to try:

- **Encourage frequent praise from leaders and peers:** At regular meetings, consider adding a few minutes for team members to praise each other at the start or end. It will feel awkward and forced at first, but once you push past that initial phase, a practice like this will normalize praise giving and receiving, and encourage everyone to actively look for those accomplishments and strengths in each other—and speak up when they see their colleagues winning.

- **Ask about celebration preferences:** Some people love being publicly recognized for their achievements, and others loathe it. Before you decide to laud a team member at a large group gathering, take them aside and ask how they'd like to be celebrated. Your introverts will thank you.

- **Celebrate internal work:** Do you have a team member who always offers to pick up birthday cakes for their colleagues? Or someone who consistently helps new hires get acclimated? Did your security ops team just thwart a minor malware attack? Heck, did Angela in accounting just fix the printer that's been driving everyone bananas? It's so easy to focus on revenue-driven goals, but small interpersonal acts of heroism and generosity deserve celebration too.

Above all, remember that these strategies and tactics aren't just about being lighthearted and fun. They're also about helping your people feel safe and accepted, enabling them to forge bonds, and encouraging them to trust themselves and each other.

"In a broader context, humor isn't jokes; it's playfulness, it's trust, it's the way that we laugh with each other. And you need a certain baseline level of trust for that to happen in the workplace," Kathy Klotz-Guest explained. "And when trust increases, humor increases. And when humor increases, trust increases. It's a virtuous cycle. If that's happening in a workplace's culture, I can tell you people there feel like they can trust each other enough to say their craziest ideas out loud."

What You Risk If You Don't Embrace Joy

Dr. W. Edwards Deming is best known for being a pioneer in quality management, but he wasn't solely focused on improving efficacy. He firmly believed that joy within workplace walls would lead to improved quality and high-performance organizations. In fact, this widely revered engineer and statistician is quoted as saying, "Management's overall aim should be to create a system in which everybody may take joy in [their] work."

Wow. Brilliant, right? A tall order, to be sure, but also a fantastic philosophy for any leader who aspires to true and ongoing compassion. If you want to foster productive, engaged teams who stick around and collaborate seamlessly, joy must be part of the equation. And it's your job to create systems that make joy possible.

Our current work culture can make that challenging.

"We tend to organize around duty," women's leadership coach Jamie Greenwood said in an interview with me.

> So what changes when we organize around joy? When we look at our day, and ask, "Oh, is that fun? No. Try and make it more fun." Joy as an organizing principle does not mean that you only do joyful things. It means you bring joy to your day, multiple times a day, so that day is just better. For instance, when I'm picking up my children and they're a mess, I bring a really yummy snack, we put on Lizzo, we tell stories. Am I still picking up my kids? Yes. Are they still having a meltdown? Yes. But I'm organizing my day around inserting joy wherever I can.

This is exactly the thinking behind why inviting a goat to your company Zoom meeting became a thing during the pandemic. People were stressed and unhappy. Their kids were doing (not doing?) school at home. They were under lockdown.

The last thing they may have wanted to do was attend an interminably long status meeting online. So smart leaders injected a bit of fun to lighten the mood and the emotional load. (You can also invite llamas, if that's what you're into.)

Leaders who ignore this Pillar of Effective Empathetic Leadership will have less joy themselves, which is bad enough, but they also risk driving their teams to exhaustion and detachment.

Since recent Gallup data shows that work friendships are strongly correlated to a long string of positive business outcomes, including improvements in profitability, safety, inventory control, and employee retention, it's likely that lonely, isolated employees will lag behind in these areas. In a piece for *Harvard Business Review*, Gallup CEO Jon Clifton wrote, "In the U.S., two in 10 workers spend a lot of the day feeling lonely. For your employees who don't have friends they can count on, work can be miserable—and that misery can make their lives worse than having no work at all."

Team members toiling away in joyless work environments are more likely to be disengaged which, over the long term, can lead to burnout, quiet quitting, or *actual* quitting. In a market where high turnover is most companies' worst fear, this is argument enough to inject some joy into the corporate culture.

Fortunately, joy comes in myriad forms. As an empathetic leader, you get to decide, along with input from your people, how you want to encourage it in your team or department. This chapter has included dozens of ideas and examples, but I want to close it out with one of my personal favorites from Steve Hartman, chief customer officer of Rugs USA. I worked with him at two previous jobs and he's also been a branding client of mine, but more importantly he's a deeply and naturally empathetic leader. In fact, when I was first kicking around the idea of writing *The Empathy Edge*, he said he'd buy copies and anonymously put them on the chairs of leaders whom he thought needed it most! The story Hartman shared is from his current company, and it's a perfect example of how simple moments of humor and joy shared by leaders can unite teams.

"We have Canned Fish Mondays," he told me.

A while back, we were talking in a meeting about the fact that everybody's eating habits have gone to hell since COVID. We have a team norm that if you're eating, you can go off camera but you need to let people know. So one time, my director of user experience and I were both going off camera and I asked, "What's for lunch?" And it turned out we were both eating sardines and crackers because that's all that was available in our houses. And after that Canned Fish Mondays became this running joke, almost like an internal meme. Things like that—these little elements of fun—can break the tension within your organization.

As we wrap up this chapter on the final Pillar of Effective Empathetic Leadership, the important thing to remember is that you don't have to be a professional comedian or a top-notch cheerleader or even a skilled event planner to bolster joy. Don't put pressure on yourself to engage in humor or dream up the perfect team-building outing from scratch. Cultivating joy isn't about creating the world's funniest work-place. It's about creating a workplace where people can relax. Because when they relax, they're more creative, they're more connected, they're more energetic, and they're more engaged.

Remember, too, that as the leader you can and should enlist others to help you up the workplace joy quotient. There are probably people on your team you can lean on—individuals who know just how to inject some energy or lighten the mood. Asking for their help will build additional engagement: when you get more team members involved, you're recruiting allies who'll contribute to maintaining a joyful culture.

If you need additional support, there are experts out there to help, such as those whom I cited in this section, Teri Schmidt of Stronger to Serve Coaching & Teambuilding whom you heard from before, and Dr. Heather Walker of Lead with Levity who offers a wonderful podcast and tailored programs designed to boost levity and increase trust and engagement. You're not alone in your pursuit of workplace joy!

The whole point of this pillar is to bring levity to your working environment because doing so builds trust. And by building trust, you are building connection and empathy. You and your team members are getting to know each other better because you're having fun and interacting outside of your daily tasks and company work.

You can start to see each other as whole human beings. As coach Jamie Greenwood so eloquently states, "Joy becomes a resilience tool because you are using it to keep going, you are using it for connection, and you are using it to remind yourself that you are not alone."

And that's going to serve you when things get complex, stressful, or challenging. Which, as all empathetic leaders know, they inevitably will.

Everyday Empathy Check-In: Joy

- What is one way I will bring joy to myself and my team today?

- Can we laugh at ourselves and our mistakes?

- How much are we talking about our personal interests, talents, and hobbies?

- Do we provide inclusive and equitable team-building and/ or socializing options to accommodate introverts, neuro-diversity, busy parents, team members with disabilities, workers of all ages, or those in recovery?

- Can we leverage tech to bring in more fun? Think video call filters or goats or llamas as guests!

- How are we celebrating mistakes as a sign of innovative risk-taking?

For more prompts and free resources to spark more joy into your work, please head to TheEmpathyDilemma.com/Resources.

Chapter Highlights

- Workplace paradigms and power structures often hinder experiences of genuine joy, trust, innovation, and collaboration, preventing authentic connections between colleagues.

- Playful facilitation methods and activities can open up team processes, encouraging creativity, empathy, and better collaboration among team members.

- Joyful environments are crucial for a great work culture and can positively impact employees' happiness, innovation, and overall well-being.

- Workplace friendships, meaningful team-building, humor, and celebration are essential tools for empathetic leaders to foster joy, trust, creativity, and cooperation.

- Neglecting joy in the workplace can lead to disengagement, burnout, detachment, and high turnover, making it imperative for leaders to prioritize and nurture joyful experiences within their teams.

WHAT'S NEXT
THE FUTURE OF EMPATHETIC LEADERSHIP

Yes, It's Bright. And No, We Won't (Completely) Outsource It to the Robots.

"I think we all have empathy.
We may not have enough courage to display it."
MAYA ANGELOU, memoirist, poet, and civil rights activist

WHEN MY BOOK *The Empathy Edge* was released in 2019, I considered it to be the business case for empathy—my argument that leaders could harness compassion as an engine for success. Back then, I never could have predicted that there would be a need for *this* book you are now reading.

Then a little thing called a "global pandemic" rolled in. And so much changed.

This book was born of a relatively new need for leaders to balance performance, people, and personal boundaries. In the years following pandemic lockdowns, company leaders began to feel like the empathy they'd extended to their people had backfired. I wanted to show them how to continue folding compassion into their policies and practices without burning themselves out or drowning in frustration. And most of all, I didn't want them to snap back to "the way things have always been" because let's be real: that old, outdated workplace culture never did any of us any favors.

And that's where we are right now: walking the line between empathy and overwhelm. But there's no doubt in my mind we won't be here forever.

So where are we headed next? What can empathetic leaders expect in the years to come? How can they cope with changing expectations about flexibility and transparency, the advent of AI, the never-ending stream of new tech, and seismic shifts in workplace dynamics?

Before I answer those questions, let me tell you a story.

How Champions Eat, Sleep, and Breathe Empathy

Steve Kerr had a brilliant fifteen-year career as an elite professional basketball player. A skilled point guard and one of the most accurate three-point shooters of all time, he helped his teams win five National Basketball Association (NBA) titles. After he retired from playing, he went on to coach the Golden State Warriors (my home team), and under his guidance, they became the first team in NBA history to win at least sixty-five games in three consecutive seasons. And they created a championship dynasty.

How does Kerr drive his teams to peak performance? Endless drilling? Threats and screaming? Bribery, shame, or badgering?

Nope: empathy.

From day one, Kerr has been very intentional about the culture and chemistry he wanted to create for the Warriors. He established the team's four core values as joy, mindfulness, compassion, and competition, and he proceeded to build a team so consistently successful it became a magnet for world-class NBA talent. (Notice how the Joy Pillar makes it in there? I'm not the only one who believes joy is crucial to healthy, empathetic, high-performing teams!)

"I think the way you build [culture] is through authenticity. And through a set of principles, the set of guiding values that you have. As a coach, you have to know what those are," Kerr said on Dr. Adam Dorsay's *SuperPsyched* podcast. "As a coach, you have to figure out who you are and what you're trying to impart to your players. Then you have to figure out how to make those values come alive each day. When they come alive through the structure and experience of each day that the players have, that's the culture. That's what they go home remembering and thinking about. And then they look forward to it the next day."

Kerr's coaching style merges his intimate knowledge of the game of basketball with his high emotional intelligence quotient, yielding a cohesive and wildly successful team. He has never sacrificed empathy and connection for high performance. Instead, his ability to balance healthy competition with genuine compassion has helped his players feel safe, supported, and driven to do their absolute best.

The culture Kerr created for the Golden State Warriors even encourages players to feel empathetic toward each other. For example, in a post-game press conference that took place after the Warriors beat the Cavaliers in the 2017 NBA championship, Warriors player Draymond Green was asked how it felt to share the win with teammates JaVale McGee and David West, both of whom were veteran players but new to the Warriors and had never won a championship.

"To see them celebrate that," he said, "was an even better feeling than just celebrating it [myself]."

Amazing, right? Kerr doesn't just walk the talk himself; he's taught his whole team to do the same. In competitive elite sports, the goal is to win. Not just perform well but actually *beat* the other team. If, in this industry, Kerr can envision and implement a compassion-based culture, teach his players to fully embody it, coach them to multiple championships, and do it all without burning himself out, corporate leaders have no excuse. They can strike a similar balance.

Surely we can manage to move forward using this new model—one that balances performance, people, and personal boundaries—and not feel so fearful of adapting to a new style of leadership. Which is actually not so new, if we think about it. Coaches like Kerr have been using this empathy-centric, boundary-friendly leadership style for decades.

Hard-driving business leaders like to cite elite athletes and coaches to rally their teams to high performance, but they're forgetting some key components: namely self-awareness, compassion, empathy, trusting relationships, and shared joy. Those components are what enable coaches like Steve Kerr to make this work—and not sacrifice their people or their performance.

It's also worth noting that empathetic leadership can be passed down from leader to leader, gradually forging a dynasty of compassion. Kerr has often attributed his coaching style to playing under and observing Phil Jackson, a longtime practitioner of Zen meditation who encouraged his teams to meditate. Jackson was also very focused on connecting with his players, understanding them as people, and maintaining compassion for the pressures of performing at such a high level. In particular, Kerr cites observing Jackson coach Dennis Rodman, a remarkably talented player with a temper and larger-than-life personality.

"The way Phil coached Dennis was the key to everything," Kerr said on the *All the Smoke* podcast. "It really informed me of what coaching was about. Because Phil demanded certain things from Dennis and got out of his way. I saw how powerful that was."

Now Kerr is inspiring a new generation of basketball coaches to steer clear of scare tactics and intimidation, embrace empathy, and *win*. This is how we exponentially impact leadership for the future. This is how we help the next generation of leaders succeed, steward their teams with care and compassion, and do so without exhausting themselves.

Many people who are excellent at the work are never taught how to actually do the job of *leading people*.

Past, Present, and Future

Setting up new leaders for success won't be easy, though, especially given the legacy of leadership that still lingers and the emerging challenges we all face.

Leadership in the past was all about command and control. You did your own job so well, you were promoted to lead others doing the same job. And so on. And so on. But many people who are excellent at the work are never taught how to actually do the job of *leading people.*

Leading people requires a different mindset, skill set, and, frankly, temperament.

As Tiffany Shlain, filmmaker, artist, and cofounder of the Webby Awards, has presciently said as far back as 2017, "The skills needed to succeed in today's world and the future are curiosity, creativity, taking initiative, multidisciplinary thinking, and empathy. These skills, interestingly, are the skills specific to human beings that machines and robots cannot do, and you can be taught to strengthen these skills through education."

Most companies know that now and focus on finding people who are equipped to mentor, strategize, build relationships, and, yes, empathize with their team members. But some companies lag behind. As I mentioned earlier, I've seen plenty of organizations pay lip service to empathetic leadership while enforcing rigid policies. Just look at Grindr, which lost 45 percent of its workforce in one week because of an unrealistic demand to get its perfectly productive and collaborative remote workforce back into the office two days a week.

"Certain leaders are snapping back to 'bossism' because they came of age in a world where there was a traditional leadership model," said Lisen Stromberg, coauthor of *Intentional Power.* "And that traditional leadership model was hierarchical and autocratic. The 'my way or the highway' philosophy. It was focused on profits at all costs, at the expense of people."

Fortunately, those leaders are in the minority now. Most successful business leaders are taking the time to get to know their teams as individuals. What motivates them, what their lives are like, who they want to become. The best of these leaders tailor communications, incentives, and career development accordingly. They invest in their people.

When I did an informal poll of executive leaders as I started writing this book, a large majority of the thirty-six respondents claimed the biggest hindrance to being more empathetic was that it takes so much time. At least that was the perception. The pausing. The listening. The tailoring. Some leaders are afraid that empathy means they now have to take the role of therapist on top of their real job, but this is not the case.

"We as leaders need to really take the time and prioritize getting to know our colleagues, the people on our teams, and our own leaders," said chief marketing officer Tracy Eiler. "But you are not a therapist. Nobody's paying you $250 an hour to just listen to them talk about boundary-setting with their mother-in-law. That's not what this is. We're asking you to be a human-centric leader."

Successful leaders know it does take time, it does take work, but they also know that doing so is quite literally their job now. And it pays off in dividends when performance and loyalty soar. "Those people will follow you to the ends of the earth and work for you again and again," adds Eiler.

If leaders want high performance and the possibility of earning bonuses for themselves, they must create a culture where people have each other's backs. These leaders recognize that doing these things isn't distracting them from the work. It *is* the work of leading.

And yet because this skill does take time and is not always the most scalable, many empathetic leaders are getting worried as more artificial intelligence applications enter our working lives. They're facing a future with some pretty overwhelming unknowns: a future where machines can take over tasks that have long been entrusted to humans, and where companies are increasingly automating everything they possibly can.

Minter Dial, author of *Heartificial Empathy*, has explored how AI is impacting leadership, specifically empathetic leadership. When I interviewed him on *The Empathy Edge* podcast, we talked about applications for AI that are actually working to create empathetic experiences for people. He pointed out that many companies are already using machine learning and AI to build more successful customer experiences, but Dial believes there are even more advanced and collaborative ways for this technology to support empathetic leaders.

"We don't have enough therapists to serve people's needs," he said. "The supply of therapists in many Western countries is just not up to the level of demand because mental health conditions have been spiraling higher and higher. Anxiety, depression, suicide, and more. Since we don't have enough therapists, I've been very keen to see certain initiatives that are designing empathic therapy through AI."

Dial added that with age demographics shifting—leaving many older people and fewer younger people—we're facing a global epidemic of loneliness. He told me he saw a world where AI could help fill the companionship void, especially in population-challenged countries like Japan. Naysayers are fearful because they want the technology to be more advanced, more refined, but he believes that waiting for imaginary benchmarks may be futile.

"People tend to hold AI to a higher standard than we hold ourselves to," he explained. "We think, 'We can't let AI do this until it's perfect.' But are we perfect? Do we do everything perfectly? If that's what we're expecting of AI, then we're never gonna get there."

In our conversation, Dial and I agreed that what we really need is to blend human touch with AI. Empathy can't just be outsourced to machines because we humans are the ones encoding the models and learnings. If some of us are still struggling to feel and practice empathy ourselves, how can we possibly program AI to do it? Instead, we need to hone our own empathetic skills, use those in our workplaces ourselves, and trust AI to take over other tasks. It can free us up to do more of the human connection work that makes our jobs so valuable.

This is good news! It means that your ability to be an empathetic leader is *critical* to creating a better future for yourself, your teams, and the leaders and teams that will follow in your footsteps.

Great strides, however, are being made to leverage cognitive AI in critical areas where more empathetic triage can be helpful when resources are stretched thin, such as healthcare guidance or university student career counseling, according to Juji CEO and founder Michelle Zhou, whom I interviewed on *The Empathy Edge* podcast. Juji is an artificial intelligence company specializing in building cognitive conversational AI technologies and solutions that enable the creation and adoption of empathetic AI agents. Cognitive AI offers cost-effective solutions to those who need guidance that adapts to their personality, learning style, and needs—something unsophisticated chatbots can't do. AI as we currently think of it can't fully replicate human connection, and it never will. And Zhou even agrees that is not quite the point.

In order to train cognitive AI models on how to accurately read and interpret different psychographic behaviors, we humans all need to get involved. "We need the domain experts to teach machines; we don't want to get IT people to teach machines," Zhou said. "That doesn't make sense, right? Because the domain experts—the counselors, the human advisors—they really know how to act upon empathy. We want them to teach machines... The current language

With this generation
at the helm, compassion
will become the
cultural model that
workers expect
across industries.

models generated by AI are actually not trying to understand individual differences. They're trying to understand the common patterns and the structures that are in the public data."

There will always be the need for us to build domain skills that effectively help us practice empathy to inform our work, our world, and our technology as it evolves.

When you leverage and fortify the Five Pillars of Effective Empathetic Leadership—self-awareness, self-care, clarity, decisiveness, and joy—you're making yourself irreplaceable. Your ability to effectively balance empathy with all the other demands will see you through these shifts, and it will even give you an advantage over others as the working world continues to evolve.

Organizational leaders of today must continue to champion empathy in balance with boundaries, compassion alongside self-care.

To me, this cycle of leadership fluctuations—from command and control to total flexibility to pervasive confusion and back to command and control—means that moving forward, we need to focus on balance. We're swinging too violently between dictatorship and anarchy. With emphasis on empathy flowing both ways, people-focused organizational leaders can usher in a new era of better collaboration, increased understanding, less entitlement, and equity on all sides.

As executive coach Ed Batista has pointed out, accountability without empathy is a boot camp. And empathy without accountability is a daycare.

Balancing the needs of the business with the needs of human employees is the best and only way forward.

Empathetic Leadership Can Start Early

The way forward can be made even easier if today's leaders start modeling and teaching empathy to younger and younger generations. I've seen the impact of this firsthand through connecting with Ed Kirwan, filmmaker and founder of Empathy Week. Kirwan is tackling the challenge of empathetic action for future generations so that maybe, just maybe, there won't be a need for empathy books like mine, because this skill will be so ingrained in our consciousness starting from a young age.

Empathy Week is an award-winning global schools program that has been run in more than forty countries; it leverages the power of film to develop the crucial skill of empathy in students aged five to eighteen. To date, it's touched the lives of more than 140,000 kids, including my own son's.

Callum's Northern California elementary school participated in 2022; kids got the opportunity to see other points of view and learn about people in Nepal who were very different from people here in the United States. Each day, students watched an age-appropriate cinematic video and engaged in discussions and activities around what they'd seen. That year, the theme was "Opportunity and Education," and the videos shown captured five different Nepalese people's lives. Beyond the films and lesson resources, Empathy Week offered an Empathy Action Project. Those who tackled this additional work divided their classes into teams who innovated solutions and made films that further developed empathy in their viewers and in themselves.

What I love about this program is it doesn't just ask kids to learn what empathy is, it invites them to practice it. Through film and carefully calibrated lesson plans and activities, Empathy Week participants learn about different cultures, lifestyles, and points of view so they can better collaborate and create belonging, developing the skills of leadership and resilience along the way.

When I spoke to Kirwan for my podcast, he told me, "If we help young people to develop empathy throughout their educational journey, they can boost understanding, reduce bias, and nurture a culture of belonging and increased well-being."

He also mentioned that many programs created to teach empathy, generosity, and selflessness to young people are too simplistic. They give out a little information, ask kids to raise money for a good cause, and leave it at that. Kirwan pointed out that this format doesn't create a real impact on the participants.

"To change the behavior of a student so that they understand another perspective, maybe someone who has a disability and can't communicate, that's way more powerful," he told me.

And I completely agree. Explaining empathy is a start, but showing kids how to model it is the best way to ensure it becomes part of their lives. I sincerely hope to see more efforts in schools to nurture empathy in young leaders, because the power of empathy in educational settings and group dynamics is tremendous.

It's a power that can build exponentially over time too. Imagine those inherently empathetic people entering the workforce, leading companies, driving change! They will come to embrace empathy as innate to their identities, and do so in a healthy, sustainable way. With this generation at the helm, compassion will become the cultural model that workers expect across industries. Those who learn empathy in elementary school now can transform leadership paradigms in just a few short years.

And we, as today's leaders, have a duty to model this and set them up for success. Which means helping them balance empathy for others with their own needs.

It's not enough for us to believe that empathy is important. It's not even enough for us to model it! We need to teach it, preach it, and pay it forward while also keeping ourselves safe and whole. We need to use the Five Pillars of Effective Empathetic Leadership so we can practice healthy empathy, support our teams, *and* achieve performance goals while still taking care of ourselves. Because if we burn out and quit, who will take up the mantle?

Successful Leaders Embrace Both/And Thinking

When you first picked up this book and read the introduction, I told you that far too many people believe empathetic leadership is an either/or proposition when it's really both/and. As business leaders, we absolutely can embrace empathy *and* ambition, compassion *and* competition, kindness *and* high performance.

But only if we have the right foundation to embrace empathy in a healthy way.

We must always remember that empathy is more about mutual understanding and support than it is about flexibility, acquiescence, or niceness. In a work setting, it means ensuring everyone understands each other, their roles and goals, and the fundamental reasons they're being asked to perform specific tasks. Without that understanding, it's easy to conflate compassion with pliability.

But *with* that understanding, we can strike that vital balance between empathetic policies and outstanding performance. We can build engaged, effective, and innovative teams who do excellent work. Happily and sustainably.

And with that balance in mind, we as leaders can also thrive and flourish in the process.

ACKNOWLEDGMENTS

I T DOESN'T ever seem fair that only one or two names get to be on a book cover. So this section is vitally important to say thank you to the many people who helped bring this book and my work to life.

Sally McGraw, my writing partner, confidante, sanity checker, and butt-kicker, thank you (again) for helping me bring another empathy book into the world. Honestly, every project is better and more fun with you on it!

Thank you to the entire publishing team at Page Two, including Jesse, Emily, Louise, Rony, Crissy, Peter, Colin, and too many others to name. You are all amazing humans. Your care and support for your authors is beyond compare. You believe in us, believe in our work. And you are always there with full hearts and open hands. Not many people can say that about their publishers!

This book would not be possible without the insights and inspirations of so many wise and wonderful practitioners you have heard from throughout this book: my *The Empathy Edge* podcast guests, as well as those I interviewed separately or whose important work I cited. Many of you I am also thrilled to call my personal friends and mentors: Amanda Carlson-Phillips, Marly Q Casanova, Dr. Robert Dodd, Tiffany Dufu,

Tracy Eiler, Rebecca Eldredge, Rhonda George-Denniston, Kat Gordon, Emily Griffin, Steve Hartman, Hilary Hendershott, Colin Hunter, Jyoti Jani, Dr. Chris L. Johnson, Amer Kaissi, Ed Kirwan, Kathy Klotz-Guest, John Kreisa, Ann Latham, Anna Liotta, Christopher Mannino, Rhonda Manns, Brandon Miller, Patrick Morrissey, Val Ries, Teri Schmidt, Michelle Sherman, Claude Silver, Lisen Stromberg, Guy Weismantel, Dave Zaboski, Michelle Zhou, and Dave Zinman. Thank you all for the work you do and for being part of the leadership and workplace transformation.

We are only as strong as those we surround ourselves with, so thank you to my Empathy Superfriends group for keeping the support and energy flowing. With all of us studying and teaching empathy from different angles, we are creating a supernova of positive change! Co-creator Rob Volpe, along with Minter Dial, Minette Norman, Anita Nowak, Edwin Rutsch, Amy J. Wilson, and too many more to name here. I appreciate every single one of you and continuously learn from your work and inspiration.

Thank you to Brianna Powell for research support, and to Gabrielle Brisbois, Dora Ozioma Ekechukwu, Alison Monday, Heather Bokon, and Lucy Moore who help me get all the things done, every day. Thanks for being on this journey with me.

Women need women who hold them up, cheer them on, make connections, and encourage them when they doubt themselves. And I am lucky enough to also call on some of these dear friends as experts in this very book because of their phenomenal work: Jonni Ressler, Rebecca Friese, Shasta Nelson, Jamie Greenwood, and Melody Biringer. And thank you to my special Authoress and Speakeress virtual communities. You all inspire me and lift me up.

Huge thanks to my family: the one I was born into, the one I married into, and the one we've created. For my mom and dad, as this is the first book of mine neither of them lived to see—yet they encouraged my writing from the tender age of five!

None of my work is possible without the love, support, and labor-sharing of my husband, Paul. You believe in me. You grill great steaks for me. You make sure we actually have groceries in the house. You have built great teams and led people with empathy and compassion yourself. You make my life better and you're not afraid to let me shine. Love you.

And for my curious, hilarious, smart, creative Callum. The best empathy practice (sparring?) partner. I hope all my stories, prayers, and antics stay with you as you get older to always be "confident, yet humble and kind." To stay curious about people who are different from you and continue to be inclusive and make friends everywhere. To be empathetic and open to other points of view. To open your heart to others with compassion *and* maintain your own well-being and boundaries. Both/And. To find joy in everything, everything, everything! I so want the world to be a better place for you, my sweet boy.

NOTES

Introduction

p. 1   *Survey Shows Dramatic Drops in Empathy among Executives:*
Jim Wilson, "Survey Shows Dramatic Drops in Empathy
among Executives," *Canadian HR Reporter*, May 18, 2023,
hrreporter.com/focus-areas/culture-and-engagement/survey
-shows-dramatic-drops-in-empathy-among-executives/376074.

p. 1   *Businessolver Study Reveals Decline in Workplace Empathy:*
Businessolver, "Businessolver Study Reveals Decline in
Workplace Empathy," PR Newswire, press release, June 21,
2022, prnewswire.com/news-releases/businessolver-study
-reveals-decline-in-workplace-empathy-301572037.html.

p. 1   *The Empathy Gap between Workers and Companies Is Bigger
Than Ever:* Shalene Gupta, "The Empathy Gap between
Workers and Companies Is Bigger Than Ever—But CEOs Just
Don't Get It," *Fast Company*, May 17, 2023, fastcompany.com/
90896561/workplace-office-empathy-ceo-employee
-disconnect-businessolver-study.

p. 1   *Fewer Workers Say Their Employer Is Empathetic in 2022:*
Ryan Golden, "Fewer Workers Say Their Employer Is
Empathetic in 2022," *HR Dive*, June 28, 2022, hrdive.com/
news/fewer-workers-say-employer-empathetic-2022/626223.

p. 3   *Workers across industries now resist workplace citizenship
behaviors:* Anthony C. Klotz and Mark C. Bolino, "When Quiet
Quitting Is Worse Than the Real Thing," *Harvard Business
Review*, September 15, 2022, hbr.org/2022/09/when-quiet
-quitting-is-worse-than-the-real-thing.

p. 3   *leaders and fully engaged workers must do more:* Naz Beheshti,
"Is a New Kind of Workaholism the Flip Side of 'Quiet

Quitting'?" *Forbes*, March 7, 2023, forbes.com/sites/naz
beheshti/2023/03/07/is-a-new-kind-of-workaholism-the
-flip-side-of-quiet-quitting.

p. 4   *iron-fist bossism, à la Elon Musk:* Kevin Roose, "Elon Musk,
Management Guru?" *New York Times*, December 16, 2022,
nytimes.com/2022/12/16/technology/elon-musk-management
-style.html.

p. 4   *"Managers need to be empathetic:* Rebecca Knight, "Companies
Can't Do Layoffs Right Because They're Trying to Act Like
'Cool Parents,'" *Business Insider*, April 13, 2023, businessinsider
.com/companies-fail-layoffs-empathetic-leadership-over-2023-4.

p. 6   *"Efficiency Is In. Is Empathy Out?":* This copy ran on the cover
of the April/May 2023 issue. Michal Lev-Ram, "Marc Benioff
Says He Can Juggle Empathy, Cost Cuts, and Layoffs as
He Doubles Down On Efficiency at Salesforce," *Fortune*,
March 30, 2023, fortune.com/longform/marc-benioff
-salesforce-cost-cuts-layoffs-acquisitions-efficiency.

Chapter 1: What Is Empathy in a Work Context?

p. 15   *Barack Obama offered a great definition of empathy:* Northwestern
University, "2006 Northwestern Commencement—Sen
Barack Obama," YouTube, June 16, 2006, youtube.com/
watch?v=2MhMRYQ9Ez8.

p. 17   *the brain's good old mirror neurons:* Leonard F. Häusser,
"Empathie und Spiegelneurone. Ein Blick auf die gegenwärtige
neuropsychologische Empathieforschung [Empathy and
Mirror Neurons: A View on Contemporary Neuropsychological
Empathy Research]," *Praxis der Kinderpsychologie und
Kinderpsychiatrie* 61, no. 5 (May 2012): 322–335, doi.org/
10.13109/prkk.2012.61.5.322.

p. 18   *It's cognitive empathy that is used in most of our interactions:*
Rob Volpe, "How Would You Answer This Question? The
State of Practicing Empathy in America: Part One," Ignite 360,
ignite-360.com/blog/the-state-of-practicing-empathy-in
-america-part-one.

p. 21   *a facilitation technique called empathy circles:* Empathy Circle
Website, empathycircle.com.

p. 25   *"If your emotional abilities aren't in hand:* Rhett Power, "High
Emotional Intelligence Is Essential in Today's Workplace," *Inc.*,
December 12, 2019, inc.com/rhett-power/high-emotional
-intelligence-is-essential-in-todays-workplace.html.

p. 25   *Self-awareness is one of the most important traits:* "Rhonda George-Denniston: Why Betting On Your People Leads to Market Domination," *The Empathy Edge with Maria Ross*, podcast episode, February 21, 2023, theempathyedge.com/ rhonda-george-denniston-why-betting-on-your-people-leads -to-market-domination.

p. 26   *It's deeply culturally uncomfortable to be kind to ourselves:* Jamie Greenwood, interview with author, 2023.

p. 28   *"People need a very clear understanding of their roles:* Dave Zinman, interview with author, 2023.

p. 30   *highlighted some of the empathetic leadership practices:* Matthew Lippincott, "Rich Hua—EI Growth at Amazon and the Tech Industry," YouTube, March 22, 2023, youtu.be/YIqVo4jvBHc.

p. 31   *when people enjoy their work:* "How Important is Job Satisfaction in Today's Workplace?" Villanova University, October 6, 2015, villanovau.com/resources/hr/importance-of-job-satisfaction -in-the-workplace.

p. 31   *happy employees mean happy customers:* Shep Hyken, "The Secret to Happy Customers," *Forbes*, February 2, 2020, forbes.com/ sites/shephyken/2020/02/02/the-secret-to-happy-customers.

p. 31   *Leaders are facing significant challenges supporting connections:* Alok Patel and Stephanie Plowman, "The Increasing Importance of a Best Friend at Work," Gallup Workplace, updated January 19, 2024, gallup.com/workplace/397058/ increasing-importance-best-friend-work.aspx.

p. 33   *banned discussion of politics at his company:* Brian Armstrong, "Coinbase Is a Mission Focused Company," Coinbase, September 27, 2020, coinbase.com/blog/coinbase-is-a -mission-focused-company.

p. 33   *quit within two weeks of the announcement:* Lila MacLellan, "Coinbase Employees Are Quitting Their Newly 'Apolitical' Workplace," *Quartz*, October 9, 2020, qz.com/work/1915278/ five-percent-of-coinbase-staff-rejected-its-apolitical-future.

p. 34   *announcing the new "apolitical" culture:* Armstrong, "Coinbase Is a Mission Focused Company."

p. 34   *Armstrong retweeting an article from Soylent founder Rob Rhinehart:* Melia Russell and Dan DeFrancesco, "Coinbase Wants to Go Public. Its CEO Needs to Change His Leadership Style First, Insiders Say," *Business Insider*, February 25, 2021, businessinsider.com/coinbase-brian-armstrong-bitcoin -cryptocurrency-profile-2020-10.

p. 34   posting a photo of himself with then speaker of the house Nancy
         Pelosi: Sandali Handagama, "Coinbase CEO Armstrong Lobbies
         US Lawmakers as Crypto Scrutiny Ramps Up," Yahoo!, May 18,
         2021, yahoo.com/video/coinbase-ceo-armstrong-lobbies
         -lawmakers-225511320.html.

p. 34   ensuring mostly high-net-worth investors could participate: Cleve
         Mesidor, "Coinbase's War On Inclusion in the Workplace,"
         Haitian Times, May 25, 2021, haitiantimes.com/2021/05/25/
         coinbases-war-on-inclusion-in-the-workplace.

p. 34   Requests for employees to delete posts questioning the "apolitical"
         policy: Gregory Barber, "The Turmoil Over 'Black Lives Matter'
         and Political Speech at Coinbase," Wired, October 5, 2020,
         wired.com/story/turmoil-black-lives-matter-political
         -speech-coinbase.

p. 34   A total of fifteen Black employees resigned: Nathaniel Popper,
         "'Tokenized': Inside Black Workers' Struggles at the King of
         Crypto Start-Ups," New York Times, November 27, 2020,
         nytimes.com/2020/11/27/technology/coinbase-cryptocurrency
         -black-employees.html.

p. 35   Leaders removed office signs that invited people to use any bathroom:
         Melia Russell, "An Incident Known as 'Bathroomgate' Left
         Some Coinbase Employees Feeling 'Targeted,' Say Former
         Workers. It's the Kind of Fight CEO Brian Armstrong Wants to
         Avoid," Business Insider, October 2, 2020, businessinsider.com/
         bathroomgate-incident-is-one-example-of-political-drama-at
         -coinbase-2020-10.

p. 35   "Black employees described feeling invisible: Barber, "The Turmoil
         Over 'Black Lives Matter.'"

p. 35   total retreat from the charged discussion: MacLellan, "Coinbase
         Employees Are Quitting Their Newly 'Apolitical' Workplace."

p. 35   "By mandating that employees keep politics, activism, and their
         personal beliefs: Laszlo Bock, "The Fallacy of the Politics-Free
         Office," Marker, October 6, 2020, marker.medium.com/
         the-fallacy-of-the-politics-free-office-bc05f10de0b8.

p. 35   turn back the clock and reinstate iron-fist bossism: Roose,
         "Elon Musk, Management Guru?"

p. 35   Looking at you, Jamie Dimon: Nidhi Pandurangi, "Jamie
         Dimon's 'Tone Deaf' Return to Office Mandate Is Getting
         Pushback from JPMorgan Staffers, Who Are Complaining
         about Being Stuck on Zoom Calls Even While in the Office:

Reuters," *Business Insider*, April 27, 2023, businessinsider.com/
return-to-office-jpmorgan-wfh-pushback-jamie-dimon-2023-4.

Chapter 2: Where We Go Wrong with Workplace Empathy

p. 40   *inappropriateness of invoking Dr. King's work in the context of
a corporate mass firing:* Alyssa Lukpat, "The CEO Who Quoted
Martin Luther King Jr. in Her Layoff Email Apologizes to
Staff," *Wall Street Journal*, January 31, 2023, wsj.com/articles/
pagerduty-ceo-jennifer-tejada-martin-luther-king-jr-quote
-layoff-email-apology-11675180388.

p. 45   *One of the colleague's team members pushed back:* Tracy Eiler,
interview with author, 2023.

p. 46   *uptick in business leaders being asked to absorb the duties of their
team members:* Rebecca Friese, interview with author, 2023.

p. 46   *20.5 million Americans were laid off:* U.S. Bureau of Labor
Statistics, "Payroll Employment Down 20.5 million in April
2020," TED: The Economics Daily, May 12, 2020, https://
www.bls.gov/opub/ted/2020/payroll-employment-down-20
-point-5-million-in-april-2020.htm.

p. 47   *4.3 million Americans quit their jobs:* U.S. Bureau of Labor
Statistics, "Job Openings and Labor Turnover Summary,"
Economic News Release, January 30, 2024, https://www
.bls.gov/news.release/jolts.nr0.htm.

p. 47   *earn the title of the Great Resignation:* Abby Vesoulis, "Why
Literally Millions of Americans Are Quitting Their Jobs," *Time*,
October 13, 2021, time.com/6106322/the-great-resignation-jobs.

p. 47   *"[Employees] don't want to return to backbreaking or boring,
low wage, sh-t jobs:* Vesoulis, "Why Literally Millions of
Americans Are Quitting Their Jobs."

p. 47   *only 23 percent of employees felt engaged at work:* Gallup, *State of
the Global Workplace: 2023 Report*, gallup.com/workplace/
349484/state-of-the-global-workplace.aspx.

p. 48   *costing the global economy $8.8 trillion in lost productivity:* Ryan
Pendell, "Employee Engagement Strategies: Fixing the World's
$8.8 Trillion Problem," Gallup Workplace, June 14, 2022, gallup
.com/workplace/393497/world-trillion-workplace-problem.aspx.

p. 48   *"Because of all the shifts:* Rebecca Friese, interview with author, 2023.

p. 48   *nearly 60 percent felt used up at the end of the workday:*
Development Dimensions International, *Global Leadership
Forecast 2021*, ddiworld.com/global-leadership-forecast-2021.

p. 48   *"Executives and leaders can be great decision-makers:* Kara
Dennison, "Executives and Leaders Are Leaving Their Roles
Due to Burnout," *Forbes,* July 28, 2022, forbes.com/sites/
karadennison/2022/07/28/executives-and-leaders-are-leaving
-their-roles-due-to-burnout.

p. 53   *Think about the things you hate doing in your day-to-day:*
"Talking Points," *Girlboss,* March 28, 2023, link.girlboss.com/
view/6410a5166d55215138503bebifxnh.i4a/939be03b.

p. 55   *We tried to do it with real empathy:* Dave Zinman, interview with
author, 2023.

Chapter 3: Generational Clashes and Other Complicating Factors

p. 61   *assumptions and stereotypes associated with your age group:* Sarah
Cottrell, "A Year-by-Year Guide to the Different Generations,"
Parents, January 30, 2024, parents.com/parenting/better
-parenting/style/generation-names-and-years-a-cheat
-sheet-for-parents.

p. 61   our belief *that they differ can impact our reactions:* Eden King,
Lisa Finkelstein, Courtney Thomas, and Abby Corrington,
"Generational Differences at Work Are Small. Thinking They're
Big Affects Our Behavior," *Harvard Business Review,* August 1,
2019, hbr.org/2019/08/generational-differences-at-work-are
-small-thinking-theyre-big-affects-our-behavior.

p. 62   *large corporations of that period felt they had enough wealth to
spread around:* Steven Pearlstein, "How the Cult of Shareholder Value Wrecked American Business," *Washington Post,*
September 9, 2013, washingtonpost.com/news/wonk/wp/
2013/09/09/how-the-cult-of-shareholder-value-wrecked
-american-business.

p. 63   *shirking their responsibility to produce returns:* Roger L. Martin,
"The Age of Customer Capitalism," *Harvard Business Review,*
January–February 2010, hbr.org/2010/01/the-age-of
-customer-capitalism.

p. 63   *getting company leadership and shareholder interests aligned:*
Martin, "The Age of Customer Capitalism."

p. 63   *There were no laws in place that forced executives:* David Kidder
and Christina Wallace, *New to Big: How Companies Can Create
Like Entrepreneurs, Invest Like VCs, and Install a Permanent
Operating System for Growth* (Currency, 2019), 14–15.

p. 64   *there are five generations in the workplace:* Elizabeth Perry,
"5 Generations in the Workplace: How to Manage Them All,"

BetterUp, August 3, 2023, betterup.com/blog/generations
-in-the-workplace.

p. 65   *more women were in the workforce than ever before:* Dan Burns
and Howard Schneider, "U.S. Employment in the 2010s in
Five Charts," Reuters, January 10, 2020, reuters.com/article/
us-usa-economy-jobs-graphic/u-s-employment-in-the-2010s
-in-five-charts-idUSKBN1Z92AK.

p. 65   *and pay rates rose:* Dr. Andrew Chamberlain, "What Happened
to Jobs Last Decade? A Look Back at the 2010s and Ahead to
2020," Glassdoor, January 7, 2020, glassdoor.com/research/
bls-predictions-december-2019.

p. 65   *more than 80 percent saw empathy as key to business success:* Jamil
Zaki, "Making Empathy Central to Your Company Culture,"
Harvard Business Review, May 30, 2019, hbr.org/2019/05/
making-empathy-central-to-your-company-culture.

p. 65   *"After years of decline, workplace empathy has improved:*
Bryan Robinson, "New Research Shows Why Business Leaders
Struggle with Workplace Empathy," *Forbes*, May 17, 2021,
forbes.com/sites/bryanrobinson/2021/05/17/new-research
-shows-why-business-leaders-struggle-with-workplace-empathy.

p. 66   *"Workers, especially younger ones, grew accustomed to:* Rebecca
Knight, "Companies Can't Do Layoffs Right Because They're
Trying to Act Like 'Cool Parents,'" *Business Insider*, April 13,
2023, businessinsider.com/companies-fail-layoffs-empathetic
-leadership-over-2023-4.

p. 66   *"There are workplace circumstances that baby boomers dreamed
about:* "Anna Liotta: Understanding Generational Codes,"
The Empathy Edge with Maria Ross, podcast episode, June 20,
2023, theempathyedge.com/anna-liotta-understanding
-generational-codes.

p. 67   *"Companies with above-average diversity produced:* Stuart
R. Levine, "Diversity Confirmed to Boost Innovation and
Financial Results," *Forbes*, January 15, 2020, forbes.com/
sites/forbesinsights/2020/01/15/diversity-confirmed-to
-boost-innovation-and-financial-results.

p. 69   *defines FGPs as being among the first persons in their immediate
family:* Baem Leadership, "First-Generation Professionals:
Today's Team Players, Tomorrow's Leaders," baemleadership
.com/first-generation-professionals.

p. 71   *First is having some kind of organizing principle:* "Tiffany Dufu:
Elevating Women through Support, Connection, and

Accountability," *The Empathy Edge with Maria Ross*, podcast episode, March 14, 2023, theempathyedge.com/tiffany-dufu -elevating-women-through-support-connection-and -accountability-2.

Chapter 4: Self-Awareness

p. 80   *"I'm an Enneagram nine, the Peacemaker:* John Kreisa, interview with author, 2023.

p. 81   *the most successful leaders understand where their natural inclinations lie:* Ginka Toegel and Jean-Louis Barsoux, "Self-Awareness: A Key to Better Leadership," *MIT Sloan Management Review*, May 7, 2012, sloanreview.mit.edu/article/self -awareness-a-key-to-better-leadership.

p. 81   *"when we see ourselves clearly:* Tasha Eurich, "What Self-Awareness Really Is (and How to Cultivate It)," *Harvard Business Review*, January 4, 2018, hbr.org/2018/01/what -self-awareness-really-is-and-how-to-cultivate-it.

p. 81   *strong financial performance had employees with higher levels of self-awareness:* "A Better Return on Self-Awareness," Korn Ferry, kornferry.com/insights/briefings-magazine/issue-17/ better-return-self-awareness.

p. 82   *In an article in* Fortune International, *Lauren Zalaznick:* Toegel and Barsoux, "Self-Awareness."

p. 86   *"Research has shown that we simply do not have access to:* Eurich, "What Self-Awareness Really Is."

p. 87   *"You really have to ask for feedback:* "Rhonda George-Denniston: Why Betting On Your People Leads to Market Domination," *The Empathy Edge with Maria Ross*, podcast episode, February 21, 2023, theempathyedge.com/rhonda-george-denniston-why -betting-on-your-people-leads-to-market-domination.

p. 89   *"I think any psychometric assessment that is effective:* "Brandon Miller: Leaders: Do You and Your Team Really Know Your Strengths?" *The Empathy Edge with Maria Ross*, podcast episode, December 20, 2022, theempathyedge.com/brandon -miller-leaders-do-you-and-your-team-really-know-your -strengths-2.

p. 89   *the MBTI tool sorts you into one of sixteen personality types:* "Myers-Briggs® Overview," Myers & Briggs Foundation, myersbriggs.org/my-mbti-personality-type/myers-briggs -overview.

p. 89   *show you how to develop your greatest talents into strengths:*
         CliftonStrengths, gallup.com/cliftonstrengths/en/254033/
         strengthsfinder.aspx.

p. 90   *help us see ourselves at a deeper, more objective level:*
         "The Traditional Enneagram," The Enneagram Institute,
         enneagraminstitute.com/the-traditional-enneagram.

p. 90   *uplevels any leader's understanding of their own twenty-first-*
         century readiness: HEARTI Leader Quotient, prismwork.com/
         hearti-leader-quotient.

p. 91   *"Brach points out that when you're having a disagreement:*
         Kat Gordon, interview with author, 2023.

p. 93   *"If you're a leader and your confidence is much higher:*
         "Amer Kaissi: Humbitious Leadership Equals Success," *The*
         Empathy Edge with Maria Ross, podcast episode, July 5, 2022,
         theempathyedge.com/amer-kaissi-humbitious-leadership
         -equals-success.

p. 93   *her techniques for creating mindful pauses and regulating*
         emotions: "Chris L. Johnson: When Leaders Pause, They Win,"
         The Empathy Edge with Maria Ross, podcast episode, September
         6, 2022, theempathyedge.com/chris-l-johnson-when-leaders
         -pause-they-win-2.

p. 94   *"You're not just walking around patting people on top of the head:*
         "John Buford & Sean Georges: On Mission Leadership,"
         The Empathy Edge with Maria Ross, podcast episode,
         December 6, 2022, theempathyedge.com/john-buford
         -sean-georges-on-mission-leadership-2.

p. 94   *The first, which we dubbed internal self-awareness:* Eurich,
         "What Self-Awareness Really Is."

p. 95   *twenty-four-point gap between how HR and CEOs view empathy:*
         "Businessolver Empathy Study Reveals a 24-Point Empathy Gap
         between HR and CEOs' Views of Each Other," BusinessSolver,
         press release, May 17, 2023, businessolver.com/news/
         businessolver-empathy-study-reveals-a-24-point-empathy-gap
         -between-hr-and-ceos-views-of-each-other.

p. 96   *"If a CEO is not self-aware, it can lead to denial:* Rae Shanahan,
         interview with author, 2023.

p. 96   *"What I've seen in the last fifteen years:* Jamie Greenwood,
         interview with author, 2023.

Chapter 5: Self-Care

p. 101   *Ardern steered her country through:* Tiffanie Turnbull, "Jacinda Ardern: New Zealand PM Quits Citing Burnout," BBC News, January 19, 2023, bbc.com/news/world-asia-64327224.

p. 102   *"I believe that leading a country is the most privileged job:* Amanda Taub, "Jacinda Ardern Says No to Burnout," *New York Times*, January 20, 2023, nytimes.com/2023/01/20/world/asia/ jacinda-ardern-burnout.html.

p. 102   *cite exhaustion and burnout as the reason for stepping back:* Kelyn Soong, "Jacinda Ardern Resignation Spotlights Burnout. Here's How to Cope," *Washington Post*, January 19, 2023, washingtonpost.com/wellness/2023/01/19/work-burnout -stress-exhaustion.

p. 102   *Gymnast Simone Biles withdrew:* Mandalit del Barco, "Simone Biles Highlights the Unique Stresses Athletes Feel at the Tokyo Olympics," NPR, July 28, 2021, npr.org/sections/ tokyo-olympics-live-updates/2021/07/28/1021670837/ simone-biles-tokyo-olympics-mental-health.

p. 102   *saw their CEOs resign:* Kara Dennison, "Executives and Leaders Are Leaving Their Roles Due to Burnout," *Forbes*, July 28, 2022, forbes.com/sites/karadennison/2022/07/28/ executives-and-leaders-are-leaving-their-roles-due-to-burnout.

p. 102   *employment-related burnout can negatively impact your mental and physical health:* Soong, "Jacinda Ardern Resignation Spotlights Burnout."

p. 102   *a staggering list of possible effects:* Monique Valcour, "Beating Burnout," *Harvard Business Review*, November 2016, hbr.org/2016/11/beating-burnout.

p. 103   *"What Jacinda has done takes enormous strength and courage:* "Dealing With Burnout: Why Jacinda Ardern's Resignation Took Enormous Strength and Courage," *Harper's Bazaar*, January 20, 2023, harpersbazaar.com/uk/beauty/mind-body/a42585513/ burnout-jacinda-ardern-resignation.

p. 104   *Executive coach Monique Valcour recommends:* Valcour, "Beating Burnout."

p. 105   *"We're squeezing these managers:* Kat Gordon, interview with author, 2023.

p. 105   *highlights the voices of business leaders who are feeling the pinch:* Businessolver, *2023 State of Workplace Empathy Report*, businessolver.com/workplace-empathy.

p. 105 *"Boundaries are a prerequisite:* Brené Brown, *Atlas of the Heart: Mapping Meaningful Connection and the Language of Human Experience* (Random House, 2021).

p. 106 *"Boundaries are the distance:* Prentis Hemphill (@pretishemphill), "Boundaries are the distance..." Instagram, April 5, 2021, instagram.com/p/CNSzFOIA2IC.

p. 106 *long hours, relentless stress, and interpersonal drama:* Tanya Ahmed, "The Bizarre Truth behind Leadership Burnout in 2024," Vantage Circle, January 3, 2024, blog.vantagecircle.com/leadership-burnout.

p. 106 *ability to engage in self-care can protect leaders:* CAO Office, "Thrive Tip: Tips to Care for Yourself When You're Experiencing Burnout," Washington University in St. Louis Human Resources, February 8, 2022, hr.wustl.edu/tips-to-care-for-yourself-when-youre-experiencing-burnout.

p. 106 *chronic stress can impact cognition:* Deirdre McPhillips, "Stress May Lead to Lower Cognitive Function, Study Finds," CNN Health, March 7, 2023, cnn.com/2023/03/07/health/high-stress-lower-cognition-study-wellness/index.html.

p. 106 *moods and attitudes are contagious:* Wharton@Work, "Leadership Influence: Controlling Emotional Contagion," The Wharton School, University of Pennsylvania, April 2021, executiveeducation.wharton.upenn.edu/thought-leadership/wharton-at-work/2021/04/control-emotional-contagion.

p. 108 *"If I am not making time for myself:* Guy Weismantel, interview with author, 2023.

p. 109 *establishing both short-term and long-term self-care practices:* CAO Office, "Thrive Tip: Reframe Your Self-Care Habits for the New Year," Washington University in St. Louis Human Resources, January 10, 2022, hr.wustl.edu/reframe-your-self-care-habits-for-the-new-year.

p. 110 *"I want to be just like Gary:* "Claude Silver: Leading with Heart at Vayner Media," *The Empathy Edge with Maria Ross*, podcast episode, July 18, 2023, theempathyedge.com/claude-silver-leading-with-heart-at-vayner-media.

p. 110 *"We're no longer in touch with who we are:* "Minter Dial: How Being Yourself Makes You a Better Leader," *The Empathy Edge with Maria Ross*, podcast episode, September 14, 2021, theempathyedge.com/minter-dial-how-being-yourself-makes-you-a-better-leader-2.

p. 113 *"[Peer support groups] allow participants to:* Boris Groysberg and
Robert Russman Halperin, "How to Get the Most Out of Peer
Support Groups," *Harvard Business Review*, May–June 2022,
hbr.org/2022/05/how-to-get-the-most-out-of-peer
-support-groups.

p. 114 *practices with proven health benefits:* Heather Cherry, "The
Benefits of Resting and How to Unplug in a Busy World," *Forbes*,
January 15, 2021, forbes.com/sites/womensmedia/2021/01/15/
the-benefits-of-resting-and-how-to-unplug-in-a-busy-world.

p. 114 *"Historically, leaders had to show their commitment:* Dave Zinman,
interview with author, 2023.

p. 116 *engaging in a pastime you truly enjoy can result in:* Emma
Parkhurst, "How Hobbies Improve Mental Health," Utah
State University, Mental Health Education Extension,
October 25, 2021, extension.usu.edu/mentalhealth/articles/
how-hobbies-improve-mental-health.

p. 116 *"Manicures and massages aren't self-care:* Jamie Greenwood,
interview with author, 2023.

p. 116 *self-care practices support your health and growth:*
Deanna Zandt, "The Unspoken Complexity of 'Self-Care,'"
Medium, October 17, 2019, medium.com/@deanna/the
-unspoken-complexity-of-self-care-8c9f30233467.

p. 117 *"When we experience stress for an extended time:* Heather Cherry,
"3 Tips for Leaders to Avoid Burnout during Stressful Times,"
Forbes, December 22, 2022, forbes.com/sites/womensmedia/
2022/12/22/3-tips-for-leaders-to-avoid-burnout-during
-stressful-times.

p. 117 *possible side effects of chronic stress and burnout:* Mayo Clinic,
"Stress Symptoms: Effects On Your Body and Behavior,"
August 10, 2023, mayoclinic.org/healthy-lifestyle/stress
-management/in-depth/stress-symptoms/art-20050987.

p. 117 *"When we think about what it takes to be at our best:* Amanda
Carlson-Phillips, interview with author, 2023.

p. 118 *"Being empathetic doesn't mean giving people everything they want:*
Rebecca Friese, interview with author, 2023.

Chapter 6: Clarity

p. 124 *"Just yesterday I read an email that was super inflammatory:* Jonni
Ressler, interview with author, 2023.

p. 125 *encounter communication breakdowns that lead to: Communication
Barriers in the Modern Workplace,* The Economist Intelligence

Unit, 2018, impact.economist.com/perspectives/sites/default/
files/EIU_Lucidchart-Communication%20barriers%20in%20
the%20modern%20workplace.pdf.

p. 126 *believe effective communication has increased their team's
productivity:* "The State of Business Communication: New
Threats and Opportunities," Grammarly, February 21, 2023,
grammarly.com/business/learn/state-of-business
-communications-2023.

p. 126 *ability to get work done is tied to how well their collaborators
communicate:* "The State of Business Communication,"
Grammarly.

p. 129 *employees value managers who are: Trust in the Modern Workplace,*
Workforce Institute at UKG, 2020, workforceinstitute.org/wp
-content/uploads/Trust-in-the-Modern-Workplace-Final.pdf.

p. 130 *"Many people think setting a boundary means:* Jamie Greenwood,
interview with author, 2023.

p. 130 *"The definition of clarity is:* "Ann Latham: The Power of Clarity,"
The Empathy Edge with Maria Ross, podcast episode, June 7,
2022, theempathyedge.com/ann-latham-the-power-of-clarity.

p. 133 *approach for virtually any issue that requires amassing and filtering
input:* Janice Fraser and Jason Fraser, *Farther, Faster, and Far Less
Drama: How to Reduce Stress and Make Extraordinary Progress
Wherever You Lead* (Matt Holt, 2021), 149–156.

p. 134 *"As leaders, we actually have to be far more explicit:* "Anna Liotta:
Understanding Generational Codes," *The Empathy Edge with
Maria Ross,* podcast episode, June 20, 2023, theempathyedge
.com/anna-liotta-understanding-generational-codes.

p. 134 *suggests crafting a code of conduct:* Michelle Sherman, interview
with author, 2023.

p. 137 *"At our company, we are very, very clear:* "Claude Silver: Leading
with Heart at Vayner Media," *The Empathy Edge with Maria
Ross,* podcast episode, July 18, 2023, theempathyedge.com/
claude-silver-leading-with-heart-at-vayner-media.

p. 138 *"If your boss comes to you and says:* Nancy Duarte, "Good
Leadership Is about Communicating 'Why,'" *Harvard Business
Review,* May 6, 2020, hbr.org/2020/05/good-leadership-is
-about-communicating-why.

p. 141 *"People don't realize that it's the question:* "Ann Latham: The Power
of Clarity."

p. 141 *great way to deliver clear, compassionate feedback:* "Colin Hunter:
Disruptive Leadership and Being More Wrong," *The Empathy*

Edge with Maria Ross, podcast episode, July 4, 2023, theempathyedge.com/colin-hunter-disruptive-leadership -and-being-more-wrong.

p. 141   *this sequence of steps for framing and asking useful questions:* Ed Batista, "Accountability and Empathy (Are Not Mutually Exclusive)," Ed Batista Executive Coaching, April 14, 2019, https://www.edbatista.com/2019/04/accountability-and -empathy.html.

p. 142   *"At an off-site, my team:* "Colin Hunter: Disruptive Leadership and Being More Wrong."

p. 143   *"Clarity and setting expectations:* Hilary Hendershott, interview with author, 2023.

p. 143   *43 percent of workers estimate they waste two weeks:* Jordan Christiansen, "Costly Conversations: How Lack of Communication Is Costing Organizations Thousands in Revenue," Crucial Learning, press release, February 3, 2022, cruciallearning.com/press/costly-conversations-how-lack-of -communication-is-costing-organizations-thousands-in-revenue.

p. 144   *"When people don't feel seen, heard, or valued:* Dave Zinman, interview with author, 2023.

p. 144   *"Under the model of policing I learned:* Christopher Mannino, interview with author, 2023.

p. 145   *"In the absence of information:* Rebecca Friese, *The Good Culture: The Leader's Guide to Creating a Workplace That Doesn't Suck* (FLYN, 2020), 39.

p. 146   *"We are still in a state of flux:* Maynard Webb, "Help! I am being forced to return to the office full time but I don't want to go back. What can I do?" LinkedIn post, March 22, 2023, linkedin.com/pulse/help-i-am-being-forced-return-office-full -time-dont-want-maynard-webb.

p. 146   *Brené Brown says, "Clear is kind. Unclear is unkind.":* Brené Brown, "Clear Is Kind. Unclear Is Unkind," Brené Brown, October 15, 2018, brenebrown.com/articles/2018/10/15/ clear-is-kind-unclear-is-unkind.

Chapter 7: Decisiveness

p. 153   *I know leaders who have been too slow to act:* Patrick Morrissey, interview with author, 2023.

p. 153   *spending more than 30 percent of their working time on decision-making:* Iskandar Aminov, Aaron De Smet, Gregor Jost, and

David Mendelsohn, "Decision Making in the Age of Urgency," McKinsey & Company, April 30, 2019, mckinsey.com/ capabilities/people-and-organizational-performance/our -insights/decision-making-in-the-age-of-urgency.

p. 154   *spent between 40 and 100 percent of their time making decisions!:* Signal AI, *The State of Decision Making Report 2021,* August 6, 2021, signal-ai.com/blog/the-state-of-decision-making -report-2021.

p. 154   *decision-making can lead to stress and fatigue:* "How Stress Impacts Decision Making," Walden University, waldenu.edu/ online-masters-programs/ms-in-clinical-mental-health -counseling/resource/how-stress-impacts-decision-making.

p. 154   *"On average, respondents spend 37 percent of their time making decisions:* Aminov, De Smet, Jost, and Mendelsohn, "Decision Making in the Age of Urgency."

p. 154   *"Picking some non-negotiables early on:* Jonni Ressler, interview with author, 2023.

p. 155   *"It's my job to make this team run well:* Tracy Eiler, interview with author, 2023.

p. 155   *"They're avoiding difficult conversations:* Val Ries, interview with author, 2023.

p. 156   *the care and compassion I received as a patient there impacted me deeply:* Maria Ross, *The Empathy Edge: Harnessing the Value of Compassion as an Engine for Success (A Playbook for Brands, Leaders, and Teams)* (Page Two, 2019).

p. 157   *"My empathy is to always understand:* Dr. Robert Dodd, interview with author, 2023.

p. 158   *"The best leaders are able to be there for their teams:* Amanda Carlson-Phillips, interview with author, 2023.

p. 160   *"You could argue decision-making is:* "Ann Latham: The Power of Clarity," *The Empathy Edge with Maria Ross,* podcast episode, June 7, 2022, theempathyedge.com/ann-latham-the-power-of-clarity.

p. 160   *"Being decisive and operating with a sense of urgency:* Steve Hartman, interview with author, 2023.

p. 161   *"Too many people see empathy and decisiveness:* "Dr. Rebecca Eldredge: Helping Leaders Manage Burnout, Overwhelm, and Compassion Fatigue," *The Empathy Edge with Maria Ross,* podcast episode, October 31, 2023, theempathyedge.com/ dr-rebecca-eldredge-helping-leaders-manage-burnout -overwhelm-and-compassion-fatigue.

p. 164   *getting in the habit of setting deadlines for decisions:* Jennifer
         Alsever, "Your Ultimate Decision-Making Guide to Help You
         Make Better Choices Faster," *Fast Company*, October 30, 2023,
         fastcompany.com/90760170/this-step-by-step-guide-will-help
         -you-make-better-decisions-faster.

p. 167   *"As a leader, you need to leave your ego behind:* Guy Weismantel,
         interview with author, 2023.

p. 169   *where people bring their ideas to a group:* "CO-STORM™,"
         womenintechregatta.com/costorm.

p. 169   *"Empathy is what you're going to apply:* Rob Volpe, interview with
         author, 2023.

p. 170   *"In these trainings, we're taught to:* Christopher Mannino,
         interview with author, 2023.

p. 171   *"As hard as it is, you learn how:* Rhonda Manns, interview with
         author, 2023.

p. 172   *"So often, I've had folks just thank me:* Tracy Eiler, interview with
         author, 2023.

p. 172   *You can be super empathetic:* Guy Weismantel, interview with
         author, 2023.

Chapter 8: Joy

p. 178   *"We recognized that all of us are playful creatures:* "Jyoti Patel and
         Emily Griffin: Let's Play More at Work!" *The Empathy Edge
         with Maria Ross*, podcast episode, December 21, 2021,
         theempathyedge.com/jyoti-patel-and-emily-griffin-lets
         -play-more-at-work.

p. 180   *surface attempt at building a joyful culture:* Rebecca Friese,
         interview with author, 2023.

p. 180   *"81 percent of employees at companies ranked:* Bob Nelson, "Why
         Work Should Be Fun," *Harvard Business Review*, May 2, 2022,
         hbr.org/2022/05/why-work-should-be-fun.

p. 180   *27 percent of someone's overall life happiness can be explained
         by:* "Remote Work Is Linked to Happiness: Study of 12,455
         Respondents," Tracking Happiness, June 18, 2023,
         trackinghappiness.com/remote-work-leads-to-happiness-study.

p. 181   *"In our 2021 survey, 61 percent of people felt less joy:* Alex Liu and
         Beth Bovis, "Joy in the New Era of Work," Kearney, April 27,
         2022, kearney.com/service/leadership-change-organization/
         article/-/insights/joy-in-the-new-era-of-work.

p. 181   *a positive correlation between how much fun people have at work:*
         Erin R. Fluegge-Woolf, "Play Hard, Work Hard: Fun at Work

and Job Performance," *Management Research Review* 37, no. 8 (2014): 682–705, doi.org/10.1108/MRR-11-2012-0252.

p. 183 *"There are a number of benefits to:* "Jyoti Patel and Emily Griffin: Let's Play More at Work!"

p. 183 *experiencing joy or other positive emotions can help protect us from burnout:* Elizabeth A. Kelsey, "Joy in the Workplace: The Mayo Clinic Experience," *American Journal of Lifestyle Medicine* 17, no. 3 (August 2021): 413–417, doi.org/10.1177/15598276211036886.

p. 183 *"According to prominent social psychologist Barbara Fredrickson:* Sophie Cliff, "How Joy Can Help Us Tackle Burnout," *Spirituality + Health*, spiritualityhealth.com/how-joy-can-help-burnout.

p. 186 *"If we can take some of the things that make improv teams:* "Kathy Klotz-Guest—Trust, Improv, & Humor for a More Innovative Culture," *The Empathy Edge with Maria Ross*, podcast episode, October 6, 2020, theempathyedge.com/kathy-klotz-guest-trust-improv-humor-for-a-more-innovative-culture.

p. 186 *"I know this one is kind of goofy:* Jackie Colburn, "More Icebreakers You Can Steal for Better Meetings," January 2023, jackiecolburn.com/blog/zkaaox5jha23harkbfslwy5li68rfy.

p. 187 *leaders with a sense of humor are viewed as 27 percent more motivating:* Jennifer Aaker and Naomi Bagdonas, "How to Be Funny at Work," *Harvard Business Review*, February 5, 2021, hbr.org/2021/02/how-to-be-funny-at-work.

p. 187 *"One great way to bring joy:* Patrick Morrissey, interview with author, 2023.

p. 188 *"In order for there to be joy:* Michelle Sherman, interview with author, 2023.

p. 189 *Forcing yourself to clown never goes well:* Naomi Bagdonas and Dick Costolo both quoted in Corinne Purtill, "How to Laugh at Work," *New York Times*, March 6, 2021, nytimes.com/2021/03/06/business/dealbook/humor-seriously-work.html.

p. 189 *"A lot of what I do is facilitating conversation:* "Kathy Klotz-Guest—Trust, Improv, & Humor for a More Innovative Culture."

p. 190 *"Here we are in Spain, Dracula" may be a tough setup:* Tina Fey, *Bossypants* (Little, Brown, 2011).

p. 190 *"Start listening, listening, listening, listening:* "Kathy Klotz-Guest—Trust, Improv, & Humor for a More Innovative Culture."

p. 190 *The average person spends 81,396 hours:* Jon Clifton, "The Power of Work Friends," *Harvard Business Review*, October 7, 2022, hbr.org/2022/10/the-power-of-work-friends.

p. 190   *having friends in the workplace doesn't only boost job satisfaction and performance:* Jamie Ducharme, "Why Work Friends Are Crucial for Your Health," *Time,* April 26, 2023, time.com/ 6274502/work-friends-health-benefits.

p. 191   *"You need leaders to say being personal with each other:* Rhitu Chatterjee, "Friendships at Work Can Boost Happiness. Here's How to Nurture Them," NPR Life Kit, February 24, 2023, npr .org/sections/health-shots/2023/02/24/1158881773/friend ships-at-work-can-boost-happiness-heres-how-to-nurture-them.

p. 191   *"In a workplace, everybody should at least be:* "Shasta Nelson: Why Successful Leaders Encourage Work Friendships," *The Empathy Edge with Maria Ross,* podcast episode, October 10, 2023, theempathyedge.com/shasta-nelson-why-successful -leaders-encourage-work-friendships.

p. 192   *assigning buddies or mentors to new hires can help them:* Clifton, "The Power of Work Friends."

p. 192   *"I have always appreciated the efforts:* Patrick Morrissey, interview with author, 2023.

p. 193   *help everyone build important interpersonal skills:* "Teri Schmidt: Empathy-Infused Team Building for Lasting Impact," *The Empathy Edge with Maria Ross,* podcast episode, September 12, 2023, theempathyedge.com/teri-schmidt-empathy-infused -team-building-for-lasting-impact.

p. 195   *people who feel recognized are more than twice as likely to bring new ideas:* Claire Hastwell, "Creating a Culture of Recognition," Great Place to Work, March 2, 2023, greatplacetowork.com/ resources/blog/creating-a-culture-of-recognition.

p. 196   *"In a broader context, humor isn't jokes:* "Kathy Klotz-Guest— Trust, Improv, & Humor for a More Innovative Culture."

p. 197   *"Management's overall aim should be to:* Lawrence M. Miller, "Dr. Deming's Joy at Work, Happiness & the High Performance Organization," *Industry Week,* March 26, 2013, industryweek .com/talent/engagement/article/21960253/dr-demings-joy-at -work-happiness-the-high-performance-organization.

p. 197   *"We tend to organize around duty:* Jamie Greenwood, interview with author, 2023.

p. 197   *why inviting a goat to your company Zoom meeting became a thing:* Sydney Page, "The Latest Thing on Zoom Meetings: A Live Goat," *Washington Post,* February 5, 2021, washingtonpost.com/ lifestyle/2021/02/05/goat-zoom-meeting-surprise.

p. 198 *"In the U.S., two in 10 workers spend:* Clifton, "The Power of Work Friends."

p. 199 *"We have Canned Fish Mondays:* Steve Hartman, interview with author, 2023.

p. 200 *offers a wonderful podcast and tailored programs:* Lead with Levity, leadwithlevity.com.

p. 200 *"Joy becomes a resilience tool:* Jamie Greenwood, interview with author, 2023.

What's Next: The Future of Empathetic Leadership

p. 206 *Steve Kerr had a brilliant fifteen-year career:* "Steve Kerr," Premiere Speakers Bureau, premierespeakers.com/ steve-kerr/bio.

p. 206 *"I think the way you build [culture] is through authenticity:* "#24 Golden State Warriors Head Coach Steve Kerr | Winning through Competition, Compassion, Joy, and Mindfulness," *SuperPsyched with Dr. Adam Dorsay,* podcast episode, July 2020, youtube.com/watch?v=IXZJxHP-dKA.

p. 207 *"To see them celebrate that:* Jason Marsh, "Three Greater Good Lessons from the Golden State Warriors," *Greater Good Magazine,* June 14, 2017, greatergood.berkeley.edu/article/item/ three_greater_good_lessons_from_the_golden_state_warriors.

p. 208 *attributed his coaching style to playing under and observing Phil Jackson:* Mihoyo Fuji, "Phil Jackson, the Zen Master of the NBA," *Zero = abundance,* April 28, 2020, interactiongreen.com/ phil-jackson-the-zen-master-of-the-nba.

p. 208 *"The way Phil coached Dennis was the key to everything:* Virgil Villanueva, "'The Way Phil Coached Dennis Was Genius'— Steve Kerr on How Phil Jackson's Methods on Dennis Rodman Helped His Career as a Coach," *Basketball Network,* January 2, 2023, basketballnetwork.net/old-school/the-way-phil-coached -dennis-was-genius-steve-kerr-on-how-phil-jacksons-methods -on-dennis-rodman-helped-his-career-as-a-coach.

p. 210 *"The skills needed to succeed in today's world and the future are:* Lee Rainie and Janna Anderson, "The Future of Jobs and Jobs Training," Pew Research Center, May 3, 2017, pewresearch.org/ internet/2017/05/03/the-future-of-jobs-and-jobs-training.

p. 210 *lost 45 percent of its workforce in one week:* Natalie Lung, "Grindr Loses Almost Half Its Staff on 2-Day RTO Requirement," *Bloomberg,* September 7, 2023,

bloomberg.com/news/articles/2023-09-07/grindr-loses-nearly
-half-its-staff-to-strict-return-to-office-rule.

p. 210 *"Certain leaders are snapping back to:* Lisen Stromberg, interview
with author, 2023.

p. 211 *"We as leaders need to really take the time:* Tracy Eiler, interview
with author, 2023.

p. 212 *"We don't have enough therapists:* "Minter Dial: How to Embed
More Heart into AI," *The Empathy Edge with Maria Ross,*
podcast episode, January 16, 2024, theempathyedge.com/
minter-dial-how-to-embed-more-heart-into-ai.

p. 213 *"We need the domain experts to teach machines:* "Dr. Michelle
Zhou: Empathic AI Is Real and It's Here—but We Need
Everyone Involved!" *The Empathy Edge with Maria Ross,*
podcast episode, November 7, 2023, theempathyedge.com/
dr-michelle-zhou-empathic-ai-is-real-and-its-here-but-we
-need-everyone-involved.

p. 215 *accountability without empathy is a boot camp:* Ed Batista,
"Accountability and Empathy (Are Not Mutually Exclusive),"
Ed Batista Executive Coaching, April 14, 2019, https://www
.edbatista.com/2019/04/accountability-and-empathy.html.

p. 216 *touched the lives of more than 140,000 kids:* "About Me," Ed
Kirwan, edkirwan.co.uk/about.

p. 217 *"If we help young people to develop empathy:* "Ed Kirwan:
Empathy Week: Using the Power of Film to Build Empathy,"
The Empathy Edge with Maria Ross, podcast episode, February 7,
2023, theempathyedge.com/ed-kirwan-empathy-week-using
-the-power-of-film-to-build-empathy.

FURTHER READING

CONTINUE YOUR journey toward empathetic leadership, culture, brands—and existence—with these wonderful books.

Alphabet Soup: The Essential Guide to LGBTQ2+ Inclusion at Work by Michael Bach (Page Two, 2022)

Applied Empathy: The New Language of Leadership by Michael Ventura (Atria Books, 2018)

The Art of Empathy: A Complete Guide to Life's Most Essential Skill by Karla McLaren (Sounds True, 2013)

Atlas of the Heart: Mapping Meaningful Connection and the Language of Human Experience by Brené Brown (Random House, 2021)

Be More Wrong: How Failure Makes You an Outstanding Leader by Colin Hunter (Page Two, 2021)

Better Allies: Everyday Actions to Create Inclusive, Engaging Workplaces by Karen Catlin (Better Allies Press, 2019)

Birds of All Feathers: Doing Diversity and Inclusion Right by Michael Bach (Page Two, 2020)

The Boldly Inclusive Leader: Transform Your Workplace (and the World) by Valuing the Differences Within by Minette Norman (BrainTrust Ink, 2023)

Bossypants by Tina Fey (Little, Brown, 2011)

The Business of Friendship: Making the Most of Our Relationships Where We Spend Most of Our Time by Shasta Nelson (HarperCollins Leadership, 2020)

Chief Inspiration Officer: How to Lead the Team Everyone Wants to Be On by Val Ries (Amplify Publishing, 2021)

Emotional Intelligence: Why It Can Matter More Than IQ (10th Anniversary Edition) by Daniel Goleman (Bantam Books, 2005)

The Empathetic Workplace: 5 Steps to a Compassionate, Calm, and Confident Response to Trauma on the Job by Katharine Manning (HarperCollins Leadership, 2021)

Empathic Leadership: Lessons from Elite Sport by Peter Sear (Routledge, 2023)

Empathy by Harvard Business Review, Daniel Goleman, Annie McKee, Adam Waytz, et al. (Harvard Business Review Press, 2017)

Empathy: A History by Susan Lanzoni (Yale University Press, 2018)

Empathy: A Lazy Person's Guide by Lou Agosta (self-published, 2020)

The Empathy Advantage: Coaching Children to Be Kind, Respectful, and Successful by Lynne Azarchi, with Larry Hanover (Rowman & Littlefield, 2020)

The Empathy Advantage: Leading the Empowered Workforce by Heather E. McGowan and Chris Shipley (Wiley, 2023)

Empathy and Morality edited by Heidi L. Maibom (Oxford University Press, 2014)

The Empathy Edge: Harnessing the Value of Compassion as an Engine for Success (A Playbook for Brands, Leaders, and Teams) by Maria Ross (Page Two, 2019)

The Empathy Effect: 7 Neuroscience-Based Keys for Transforming the Way We Live, Love, Work, and Connect across Differences by Helen Riess, with Liz Neporent (Sounds True, 2018)

The Empathy Factor: Your Competitive Advantage for Personal, Team, and Business Success by Marie R. Miyashiro (PuddleDancer Press, 2011)

Empathy for Change: How to Create a More Understanding World by Amy J. Wilson (New Degree Press, 2021)

Empathy in Action: How to Deliver Great Customer Experiences at Scale by Tony Bates and Dr. Natalie Petouhoff (Ideapress Publishing, 2022)

Empathy in the Global World: An Intercultural Perspective by Carolyn Calloway-Thomas (SAGE Publications, 2010)

Empathy Unchained: Heal Your Trauma, Uplift the World by Felicia Darling (GracePoint Publishing, 2024)

Empathy Works: The Key to Competitive Advantage in the New Era of Work by A. Sophie Wade (Page Two, 2022)

Entangled Empathy: An Alternative Ethic for Our Relationships with Animals by Lori Gruen (Lantern Publishing & Media, 2015)

The E Suite: Empathetic Leadership for the Next Generation of Executives by Tina Kuhn and Neal Frick (Greenleaf Book Group Press, 2023)

Farther, Faster, and Far Less Drama: How to Reduce Stress and Make Extraordinary Progress Wherever You Lead by Janice Fraser and Jason Fraser (Matt Holt, 2021)

The Future of Feeling: Building Empathy in a Tech-Obsessed World by
   Kaitlin Ugolik Phillips (Little A, 2020)
*The Genius of Empathy: Practical Skills to Heal Your Sensitive Self, Your
   Relationships, and the World* by Judith Orloff (Sounds True, 2024)
*The Good Culture: The Leader's Guide to Creating a Workplace That
   Doesn't Suck* by Rebecca Friese (FLYN, 2020)
Heartificial Empathy: Putting Heart into Business and Artificial Intelligence
   (2nd edition) by Minter Dial (DigitalProof Press, 2023)
Humbitious: The Power of Low-Ego, High-Drive Leadership by Amer
   Kaissi (Page Two, 2022)
Humor, Seriously: Why Humor Is a Secret Weapon in Business and in Life
   by Jennifer Aaker and Naomi Bagdonas (Currency, 2021)
Intellectual Empathy: Critical Thinking for Social Justice by Maureen
   Linker (University of Michigan Press, 2014)
*Intentional Power: The 6 Essential Leadership Skills for Triple Bottom Line
   Impact* by Lisen Stromberg , JeanAnn Nichols, and Corey Jones
   (Wiley, 2023)
*The Leadership Pause: Sharpen Your Attention, Deepen Your Presence, and
   Navigate the Future* by Chris L. Johnson (BrainInk Trust, 2022)
Leading with Empathy: Understanding the Needs of Today's Workforce by
   Gautham Pallapa (Wiley, 2021)
Listening Well: The Art of Empathic Understanding by William R. Miller
   (Wipf & Stock, 2018)
*The Moral Dimensions of Empathy: Limits and Applications in Ethical
   Theory and Practice* by Julinna C. Oxley (Palgrave Macmillan, 2011)
*New to Big: How Companies Can Create Like Entrepreneurs, Invest Like
   VCs, and Install a Permanent Operating System for Growth* by David
   Kidder and Christina Wallace (Currency, 2019)
On Mission: Your Journey to Authentic Leadership by John Buford and
   Sean Georges (Greenleaf Book Group Press, 2022)
*The Power of Clarity: Unleash the True Potential of Workplace Productivity,
   Confidence, and Empowerment* by Ann Latham (Bloomsbury
   Business, 2021)
*The Power of Empathy: A Practical Guide to Creating Intimacy, Self-
   Understanding, and Lasting Love* by Arthur Ciaramicoli and
   Katherine Ketcham (Piatkus Books, 2000)
*The Power of Empathy: A Thirty-Day Path to Personal Growth and Social
   Change* by Michael Tennant (Chronicle Books, 2023)
The Power of Kindness: Why Empathy Is Essential in Everyday Life by
   Brian Goldman (HarperCollins, 2018)

Practical Empathy: For Collaboration and Creativity in Your Work by Indi Young (Rosenfeld Media, 2015)

Practicing Empathy: Pragmatism and the Value of Relations by Mark Fagiano (Bloomsbury Academic, 2022)

The Psychological Safety Playbook: Lead More Powerfully by Being More Human by Karolin Helbig and Minette Norman (Page Two, 2023)

Purposeful Empathy: Tapping Our Hidden Superpower for Personal, Organizational, and Social Change by Anita Nowak (Broadleaf Books, 2023)

Radical Empathy: Finding a Path to Bridging Racial Divides by Terri E. Givens (Policy Press, 2021)

Radical Empathy in Leadership: Equity-Focused Testimonials, Trials, and Tools for School Leaders by Dr. Ian Roberts (self-published, 2021)

Realizing Empathy: An Inquiry into the Meaning of Making by Seung Chan Lim (self-published, 2013)

A Rumor of Empathy: Rewriting Empathy in the Context of Philosophy by Lou Agosta (Palgrave Pivot, 2014)

Social Empathy: The Art of Understanding Others by Elizabeth A. Segal (Columbia University Press, 2018)

Spark the Heart: Engineering Empathy in Your Organization by Dr. Nicole Price (Forbes Books, 2023)

Start with Why: How Great Leaders Inspire Everyone to Take Action by Simon Sinek (Portfolio, 2011)

Stop Boring Me! How to Create Kick-Ass Marketing Content, Products, and Ideas through the Power of Improv by Kathy Klotz-Guest (Keeping It Human, 2016)

The Strength of Sensitivity: Understanding Empathy for a Life of Emotional Peace & Balance by Kyra Mesich (Llewellyn Publications, 2016)

Teaching Empathy: A Blueprint for Caring, Compassion, and Community by David A. Levine (Solution Tree Press, 2005)

Tell Me More about That: Solving the Empathy Crisis One Conversation at a Time by Rob Volpe (Page Two, 2022)

Time to Listen: How Giving People Space to Speak Drives Invention and Inclusion by Indi Young (self-published, 2022)

Unlocking Generational CODES: Understanding What Makes the Generations Tick and What Ticks Them Off by Anna Liotta (Aviva Publishing, 2012)

Work Made Fun Gets Done! Easy Ways to Boost Energy, Morale, and Results by Bob Nelson and Mario Tamayo (Berrett-Koehler, 2021)

You Lead: How Being Yourself Make You a Better Leader by Minter Dial (Kogan Page, 2021)

Zero Degrees of Empathy: A New Theory of Human Cruelty by Simon Baron-Cohen (Penguin Books, 2011)

ABOUT THE AUTHOR

MARIA ROSS is a speaker, facilitator, author, strategist, and empathy advocate who believes cash flow, creativity, and compassion are not mutually exclusive. She's spent decades helping forward-thinking leaders and teams worldwide connect and engage through empathy to accelerate growth and impact. Maria has authored multiple books and hosts *The Empathy Edge* podcast.

Maria understands the power of empathy on both professional and personal levels: in 2008, shortly after launching her business, she suffered a ruptured brain aneurysm that almost killed her and inspired her memoir, *Rebooting My Brain*. In it, she explores the critical importance of empathy in healing and overcoming adversity.

Maria has appeared in many prominent media outlets, including MSNBC, NPR's *Wisdom from the Top with Guy Raz*, *Forbes*, ABC News, *Entrepreneur*, and Thrive Global. She gives powerful talks and trainings for companies such as Salesforce, TBWA\Worldwide, New York Life Insurance, and CHRISTUS Health. She's delivered dynamic keynotes at venues ranging from TEDx to the *New York Times* to the 3% Conference. Her writing has appeared in multiple publications including *Entrepreneur*, *Newsweek*, and HuffPost.

Maria lives in the San Francisco Bay Area with her husband, young son, and rescue mutt.

CONTINUE THE EMPATHY CONVERSATION

- **Listen:** *The Empathy Edge* podcast showcases innovative leaders, organizational experts, bestselling authors, and other practitioners sharing actionable advice to leverage empathy for tremendous success. Go to TheEmpathyEdge .com or follow us on your favorite podcast player.

- **Copies for your team, customers, clients, or organization:** Want to support your leaders with essential strategies and tactics to help them balance empathy and performance? You'll enjoy book volume discounts and options to customize *The Empathy Dilemma* with your brand. Please reach out to info@Red-Slice.com.

- **Bring me in!** Benefit from dynamic talks that will enrich people both personally and professionally. I offer leadership training workshops, ERG talks, and conference/event keynotes that will surprise and delight. Please reach out to info@Red-Slice.com to customize a program for your goals.

- **Review:** If you enjoyed *The Empathy Dilemma*, please leave an *honest* review online with your preferred retailer. Reviews help like-minded readers find my book because... search algorithms.

- **Newsletter:** Join thousands of other empathy enthusiasts by signing up for my weekly newsletter. Get insights and inspiration on how to strengthen empathy and build a winning team, culture, and brand. Sign up at Red-Slice.com/Newsletter.

- **Free resources:** For more prompts and free resources to help you shore up your own self-awareness, please head to TheEmpathyDilemma.com/Resources.

- **Connect on social media:** Empathy is alive and well and living online. Connect with me in the following places and let's build an Empathy Army (#EmpathyEdge).

  🌐 RedSlice.com | TheEmpathyEdge.com
  💼 linkedin.com/in/mariajross/
  📷 instagram.com/redslicemaria/
  🧵 threads.net/@redslicemaria
  🅕 facebook.com/redslice
  ▶ youtube.com/user/mariajross